Such a candle

1555.
M. HVGH LATIMER
BISHOP OF WORST.

Æ.T. 74

Hugh Latimer.
(Reproduced by courtesy of the National Portrait Gallery.)

SUCH A CANDLE

The Story of Hugh Latimer

Douglas C. Wood

 EVANGELICAL PRESS

EVANGELICAL PRESS
P.O. Box 5, Welwyn, Hertfordshire AL6 9NU, England

© Evangelical Press 1980
First published 1980

ISBN 0 85234 134 2

Cover design by Peter Wagstaff

Typeset in 11pt on 12pt Baskerville by Beaver Publishing Services Ltd,
Maidstone, Kent.
Printed in Great Britain by Halstan & Co. Ltd., Amersham, Bucks., and
bound by J. M. Dent, Letchworth.

Dedicated to
my wife Christine, without whose help, encouragement
and patience this book would not have been written.

Contents

List of illustrations

Acknowledgements

The author wishes to thank the following authors and publishers for permission to quote from their works: *Roman Catholicism* by Dr L. Boettner, published by the Presbyterian and Reformed Publishing Company, Philadelphia, Penna., U.S.A. and *Hugh Latimer* by Harold S. Darby, published by Epworth Press, London.

He also wishes to express his gratitude to his former Principal, Dr R. N. Caswell and the staff of Belfast Bible College for the years 1955 to 1957, which laid the foundations of a love for the Word of God and the history of Christ's church.

He is particularly indebted to Mr Gordon Sayer, Librarian of the Evangelical Library, London, and his staff for their help in supplying valuable books of reference for this work.

1. Soul in torment

1524

The university cross-bearer strode forward, his jaw set in a determined line. 'It must stop,' thought Hugh Latimer. The pernicious teachings of that upstart monk, Martin Luther, had been smuggled into England and, despite the efforts of Cardinal Wolsey and the Bishop of Ely, had spread in Cambridge. Why, one of the professors, Dr George Stafford, was now giving a series of lectures on the Scriptures and the hall he lectured in was crowded with students! Latimer attended one of these lectures and, while he inwardly writhed as he was forced to listen to God's Word expounded, he jumped up at the end and entreated the students not to come to any more lectures. But they had been drinking in every word of Dr Stafford's lecture and they would not listen. Latimer was rude to Professor Stafford and insisted that he was teaching heresy because he was expounding Scripture.

Latimer was not a student. He was a graduate of Cambridge and a Fellow of Clare Hall. He had been ordained as a priest some years before and had been teaching while he continued his studies for his degree as Bachelor of Divinity.

Hugh Latimer was born in about 1485 at Thurcaston in Leicestershire, just twelve miles from Lutterworth. At the time when our story opens, the so-called heresy of reading and expounding Scripture, taught by John Wycliffe at Lutterworth Rectory over 140 years before, was still rife in Leicestershire. Wycliffe had also lectured at Oxford, where he had been a Doctor of Divinity, and had maintained that the Bible should be translated into English for all to read. He had even defied the church leaders of his day and, with the help of his friends, made an English translation from the Latin Vulgate. Printing had not been introduced to England at the time but the Lollards, Wycliffe's followers, had preached from handwritten copies of his translation and this spread the 'heresy' throughout England. The Lollards [1] had been vigorously persecuted by the church and many had died at the stake. Even now, in 1524, there were still a few people who talked in the alehouses about the Lollards or 'poor priests' who had once roamed England after the rise of John Wycliffe in the thirteen-seventies.

Latimer's father had protected him from these teachings when he was a child. He tells us in his own records that no hint of Lollard sympathies was found on his father's farm in Leicestershire. It is highly probable that Hugh's father had chosen Cambridge for his son because Oxford was still regarded with suspicion by the more orthodox, owing to Wycliffe's teaching.

But had Latimer never heard anything of this teaching? As one writer has said, 'The spiritual restlessness which had found its first voice in Wycliffe a hundred years earlier was a feature of the local life. The gossip of farm-hands on the ale-bench on summer evenings, the talk of women in the churchyard after mass, wisps of idea and doctrine, of opinion and development, verses of Scripture spoken in the mother tongue, travelled without chroniclers being able to note their passage. . . . Leicestershire had remained. . . one of the counties most favourable to the doctrines Wycliffe had proclaimed by word of mouth and pen.' It is probable that some childhood memories of these things made Latimer fear the rise of a new generation of Lollards.

For him the trouble had all begun with Erasmus's translation. This was a new Latin version of the New Testament together with the Greek text. Latimer knew that a group of students met regularly in one of the taverns to study Erasmus's translation, although the meetings were so secretive that he had learnt very few details. The other students had nicknamed the tavern 'Germany' because it was suspected

---

1. Lollard, meaning 'babbler' or 'mumbler' was the sneering nickname given to Wycliffe's followers by the clergy.

that the group were studying books from the pen of Martin
Luther, the German 'heretic' who had defied the church
several years previously.

Erasmus's translation had spread like the plague through
the university and students from at least five colleges were
taking part in these meetings. Like all priests, Latimer was
opposed to any translation for the ordinary people. The
teachings of the church were adequate for them. There were
even rumours that an obscure priest, William Tyndale, was
thinking of translating the New Testament into English. This
would mean that not only students but any layman could
then read it. At least the students were all in minor orders,
that is they were counted as junior clergy, but for a layman
to handle sacred writings was dangerous for his soul. Latimer
felt that the bishops were too half-hearted in their efforts to
stamp out this new teaching. For him there was only one
punishment for the unrepentant heretic — death at the stake.
The trouble was that the king was friendly with Desiderius
Erasmus and considered himself a scholar and a patron of the
arts. King Henry's recent book *The Assertion of the Seven
Sacraments* seemed to substantiate this. It was good, in
Latimer's eyes, but after receiving the pope's blessing and
being awarded the title 'Defender of the Faith', the king had
then lost interest.

The English people, especially the peasants, had been
without even a part of the Bible for centuries. There had
never been a complete translation. The Venerable Bede had
translated John's Gospel, and Alfred, King of Wessex, had
assembled learned men around him who, in the eight hundred
and seventies, had translated the four Gospels. Alfred himself
is believed by many to have translated the first fifty psalms
into Anglo-Saxon. Other pious scholars translated fragments
of the Scriptures in the following centuries. But these translations were hidden away in the libraries of monasteries. The
teaching prevailed that the reading of the Bible was dangerous for the laity, and even the clergy thought it better to
ignore the Vulgate (the Latin version of the Bible) and con-
centrated instead on the legends of the saints. Many churches

were served only by an underpaid and semi-illiterate 'mass-priest' who barely understood the Latin words he mumbled as he said mass. 'Father John-lack-Latin' the local people might have named him.

Not that the church was poor — far from it — but the number of men who held the 'livings' of several churches, but never visited any of them, was legion. Mass must be said, of course, so they drew the money for these churches and appointed 'mass-priests', whom they paid a pittance, while they themselves either continued in idle luxury and hunting or else pursued their political careers. Italian bishops held the livings in several parts of the West Country but the only recorded visit to England of any foreign bishop in the sixteenth century is that of Cardinal Campeggio who was, among other things, Bishop of Salisbury. But when he arrived in England he did not set foot in his diocese. He came as one of the two papal legates appointed by the pope who were to decide whether King Henry's marriage was valid or not, and to discuss the possibility of a divorce.

In the fifteenth century, William Caxton, the first English printer, had a difficult choice to make before he started printing. Following the Norman Conquest, French had become the language used in court and among the nobility. Latin was the language used by the clergy and all scholars, while English, as used by the peasants, was still in a state of flux. There were almost as many dialects as there were counties of England and they were constantly changing — partly owing to the influence of French and Latin. Caxton made his choice after much thought and advice, and nearly a hundred books came from his press. So the foundations for 'literary English' were laid. English came back into its own among the upper classes. If anyone now translated the Bible into English he would have a distinct advantage over Wycliffe. But at present the only people who could taste God's Word were the students who gathered to read Erasmus's translation.

Latimer records seeing King Henry VII at Cambridge in the very year that he went up there himself (1507). As he watched the king ride past in state with the glittering crown of England on his head, Latimer remembered that this was the man for whom his father had ridden forth to fight at Blackheath when the Cornish rebels had marched across the country. He could still remember helping his father buckle on his armour and climb stiffly into the saddle while his mother and sisters stood by weeping and he thought how, as a lad of twelve years old, he had longed to go with his father.

England had been comparatively peaceful since Henry VII's accession to the throne. York had been defeated and the House of Tudor now ruled. The Wars of the Roses were over. Arthur, Henry's eldest son, who should have succeeded him, had died soon after his marriage. This marriage had also been marked by another death. Young Warwick, the last of the Plantagenets and the only possible pretender to the throne, had been confined to the Tower by Henry. Ferdinand, King of Spain, wanted to be sure that his daughter Catherine would have no opponent when she ascended the English throne. Henry's word was not enough for him. The Castilian chancellor had to be present when Warwick's head rolled on the scaffold. Only then was Catherine given as a bride to Arthur. As one historian shrewdly observes, 'The marriage of Catherine the Catholic was a marriage of blood.'

Upon Arthur's death, after it was certain that Catherine would not bear a child, Prince Henry had been declared the heir to the throne. His father, Henry VII, was covetous and did not want to return to Spain the one hundred thousand crowns that were part of Catherine's dowry. Surely there must be some way round this. Could he not wed Prince Henry to Catherine? Despite the arguments of Warham, Archbishop of Canterbury, who maintained that Scripture said a man should not take his brother's wife (Leviticus 20:21), and the Canon Law of the Roman church which forbad it, Henry was determined to try. At the suggestion of a bishop, he wrote to the pope, paid him a large sum of money and was granted a papal bull.[2] It was under this papal dispensation

2. Papal bull — a papal document bearing the command or commission of the pope and which has the papal seal (from Latin *bulla*, seal).

that Henry was married to Catherine at Greenwich, six weeks after his accession to the throne. So, when the coronation at Westminster Abbey took place on Michaelmas Day 1509, it was a double crowning.

Much had happened since then and, as Latimer walked moodily along the banks of the Cam, the only problem that occupied his mind was what could be done about these Bible lectures and the Lutheran teaching, which he was sure was spreading like a fire. His face darkened with anger as two figures walked quickly round the corner away from the icy wind that swept across from the fens. He recognized one of the men as Thomas Bilney, who had become well known at Cambridge as leader of the group of students that met at the White Horse tavern. In defiance of the church they studied and discussed the new translation into Latin of the New Testament made by the Dutch scholar Desiderius Erasmus. The group was popular and appeared to be growing daily.

Soon after this, Latimer learned that he had passed his examinations. He was now a Bachelor of Divinity. He would have to give a lecture before the whole university on a suitable subject. It is quite in keeping with Latimer's misguided zeal that he should have chosen as his theme, *Philip Melancthon and his Doctrines*. As the German Reformer, one of Luther's colleagues at Wittenberg, insisted that all teaching and ritual must be tested by the Bible, Latimer decided to stress the danger to which the students who met at the White Horse tavern were exposing their souls as they read the New Testament. Students and fellows alike must realize that all truth was held by the church.

Apart from the natural inability of any person to understand the Bible without the enlightenment of the Holy Spirit, the Scholastic[3] teaching on biblical interpretation would have blinded Latimer to the truth of Scripture. The students who met at the White Horse Tavern were doing as all the

3. Scholastics largely based their teaching on the philosophy of Thomas Aquinas (c.1225-1274) who drew many of his ideas from the teachings of Aristotle, a pagan philosopher who lived in the fourth century B.C. Scholasticism prevailed in the Middle Ages.

Cambridge: the entrance gateway to King's College, with the fifteenth century tower of Great St Mary's Church, where Latimer preached the sermon against Melancthon. *Reproduced by courtesy of Barnaby's Picture Library.*

Reformers did: they were reading Scripture literally, as this was the only way to find God's meaning.

When the great day came and Latimer entered the pulpit in Great St Mary's Church and scanned the sea of waiting faces of students, fellows and professors, he probably did not notice a small man in the midst. 'Little Bilney' was present. Even if the rules had not demanded that all students and fellows should be there, Thomas Bilney would have been present, since he had remained a good 'son of the church'. His discovery of the truth in God's Word, that had set him free from his burden of sin and which he delighted to share with others, had not made him a rebel or careless about divine service. Today, as he listened to Latimer's thunderings against Melancthon, he realized that here was zeal without knowledge. If only this man could be brought to a knowledge of the truth!

Latimer finished his discourse and there was great applause for him as he left the pulpit. 'Here is the man who will be a real "defender of the faith",' said many of the Cambridge dons. 'He can confound the German heretics and save the church. He can certainly save England and Cambridge.' Latimer was no doubt gratified by their praise: his lecture had been a success. But he was quite unprepared for the final outcome.

Bilney had been watching Latimer carefully and had seen that here was another Saul of Tarsus, full of 'zeal for God, but not enlightened'. As he watched Latimer, he thought hard and prayed for wisdom.

Shortly after his sermon in front of the university, Latimer heard a knock on his study door. When he opened it, there stood Bilney. Latimer was astonished. What could he want?

2. 'Damascus road'

1524

'For the love of God, be pleased to hear my confession,'[1] Bilney pleaded.

Latimer was astounded. The heretic wanted to make confession to the Catholic. He felt a sense of triumph.

'My sermon has converted him,' Latimer thought. 'If he returns to the church, the others will soon follow suit!'

He eagerly agreed to the request. Bilney knelt before him and he waited for the expected confession of disobedience to the church, of reading and teaching others false doctrine, and so leading them astray from the path marked out by their spiritual fathers. Instead, Bilney recounted how he had bought pardons, paid for masses and gone on pilgrimages, but all to no avail. He told Latimer of the anguish he had suffered in his soul and the uselessness of everything that the church had prescribed. He then spoke of the peace that had come to him after he had bought Erasmus's New Testament and read in its pages that Jesus Christ is the Lamb of God that takes away the sin of the world.

At first Latimer listened without mistrust — he had heard countless confessions from penitents — but as Bilney continued he became disturbed. He had expected penitence, but this was nothing but a confession of faith. He wanted to get away from Bilney, yet something in the latter's quiet simplicity commanded his attention.

It is possible that, as Bilney quoted Paul's words from 1 Timothy, a picture of one of the medieval tapestries which depicted Paul's conversion on the road to Damascus flashed through Latimer's mind and he recalled how blind the apostle

1. *Latimer's Sermons*, Parker Society, p. 334.

had been until the Holy Spirit opened the eyes of his understanding.

At length the sovereign grace of God prevailed in Latimer's
heart. Like Paul, he had been fighting against God but now
he was conquered and, like the apostle, his conversion was
instantaneous. He did not know what to say, but Bilney, who
had helped others who were seeking Christ, drew closer to
him and with his aid Latimer came into the full light of the
gospel. Latimer was horrified as he thought of all that he had
done, fighting against God. But Bilney comforted him and
pointed out that Christ's cleansing had blotted out all his
sins.

We can be sure that one of the first things that Latimer did
was buy a copy of the New Testament — the book that he
had hated and feared — to read and study for himself the
glorious truths of Scripture. 'From that time forward I began
to smell the Word of God,' Latimer said years later. 'I for-
sook the school-doctors and such fooleries.'

One of the other things that Latimer had to do was apologize to Dr Stafford for his rudeness. Not only was this forgiven, but from that time on the two became fast friends. But
Latimer's closest friend was Bilney. How much he owed to
him! He helped Bilney in his works of mercy, they prayed together and were frequently seen walking on a place near
Cambridge which came to be nicknamed, 'Heretics' Hill'.
Latimer still had many things to sort out in his mind and
these walks gave him the opportunity to discuss them privately and find out what Bilney, the more mature Christian,
had to say.

They became like David and Jonathan — inseparable.
Latimer, speaking years later, said, 'Master Bilney, or rather
Saint Bilney that suffered death for God's Word's sake, the
same Bilney was the instrument whereby God called me to
knowledge; for I may thank him, next to God, for that knowledge that I have in the Word of God. For I was as obstinate a
papist as any was in England.' When Latimer eventually
moved from Cambridge he always kept in touch with Bilney.

Thomas Bilney was born in Norfolk, near Norwich, in

about 1495 and went up to Trinity Hall, Cambridge when in
his teens. At the time he and Latimer became friends, he had
already passed his LL.B. degree and was a fellow of his
college. Although he was studying law, his main quest was
peace with God. His conscience gave him no rest and when he
went to the priests, who were supposed to care for his soul,
they appointed for him prolonged vigils, masses and pilgrimages, but none of these gave him that peace for which he
longed. He told Latimer, as they walked together, that in fear
and trembling he had bought a copy of Erasmus's translation
about five years previously. He had thumbed through the
New Testament[2] and found one of the letters written by St
Paul, where these words seemed to stand out from the page:
'It is a true saying, and worthy of all men to be embraced,
that Christ Jesus came into the world to save sinners, of
whom I am the chief and principal' (1 Timothy 1:15). As he
meditated on this verse a great peace came over him. If St
Paul could be confident, so could he. Jesus Christ could save
him, too!

But after that first wave of joy and relief, as he told
Latimer, Bilney was perplexed by the way the priests hated
and feared the New Testament. Why did they not preach this
good news from the pulpits? He had never heard it preached
in his life.

Bilney felt strongly that such wonderful news was too
good to keep to himself. He spoke to friends who had expressed an interest in Erasmus's translation and soon a small
group met regularly in Bilney's room for discussion of the
Bible. Several other students found the same peace and joy
that Bilney had sought and gradually the group grew larger as
the years passed. Later they met at the White Horse tavern as
they needed more space. Among those who joined them for a
time was William Tyndale, the young graduate who had
arrived from Oxford. He came for fellowship with other like-

---

2. The first edition of Erasmus's New Testament was produced at
Basle in 1516 but it was his second edition of 1519 that swept through
England and reached Cambridge.

minded men and to discuss the contrast between Scripture and church doctrine and practice. It is questionable if Tyndale had then formed the idea of translating the Bible into English — 'a book for the ploughboy' — but he certainly came to improve his Greek. Cambridge, thanks to Desiderius Erasmus and his three years of lectures on this language, was now the English centre for studying Greek.

While the bishops frowned and the priests stormed from the pulpit at Erasmus's work and declared Greek to be the devil's own language, students still bought the New Testament, and at the White Horse it was not only read but studied devoutly. Many other students later came to believe, either through Bilney's preaching at the tavern or through the influence of friends. It is thought that John Frith, of King's College, was converted through the influence of Tyndale. Later these two men were to be the closest of friends and Frith was to join Tyndale on the Continent for a time and help him with the translation of the Bible into English.

As Latimer and Bilney met with students in the White Horse tavern they were in fact the forerunners of today's Cambridge Inter-Collegiate Christian Union, which for over one hundred years has exercised an evangelical witness in Cambridge among students. Prayer, Bible study and a clear witness to biblical truth among fellow students were the methods used by Bilney and Latimer, and today the CICCU has proved that these are still the means most honoured and blessed by God.

Latimer was surprised at the approach to Scripture adopted by the group at the White Horse tavern. Trained as a Scholastic, he had been accustomed to regard the literal sense of a passage as unimportant and unedifying. The Scholastics declared that each portion of Scripture had three levels of meaning: broadly speaking all of them were allegorical . There was the 'moral' meaning to teach one rules of conduct, the 'allegorical' to teach one doctrine and the ana-gogical' to teach one the invisible realities of heaven. Treated in this way, the Bible was used to support many strange ideas, none of which bore any relation to the Word of

God.[3] With these peculiar ideas on the interpretation of Scripture, which they followed rigidly, it is easy to see why the hierarchy were not only fearful lest the students or the laity should read the Bible, but felt that it was safer for their own souls if they left it alone and merely reverenced it as a sacred book.

Bilney and his friends showed Latimer how they were learning from God's Word as they studied it and accepted it literally, apart from the passages which were clearly intended to be read as poetry. They had discovered that other great truth that good works do not make us righteous in God's sight but, as Tyndale later wrote, 'faith justifies us to make us fruitful in good works'. So, although they did not rely on their good works as a means of obtaining God's favour, they tried to put into practice the instructions given in the Epistles, and especially in James, on the need to perform acts of kindness and mercy. Bilney told Latimer that they were seeking to obey the New Testament teaching, and he tried to show his practical Christianity by visiting prisons and the sick, and bringing to the starving and the beggars the food he saved by his own sparse living.

The group of Reformers at Cambridge had gained a valuable addition to their number in Latimer. Older and more mature than the students and postgraduates, he was more cautious about the changes that needed to be made in doctrine and practical Christianity. As he joined in the discussions in the White Horse tavern, he acted as a restraint on those wilder influences that often appear at times of revival or reformation. 'What need have we of universities and schools?' some extremists asked. 'The Holy Ghost will always give us what to say.' Latimer insisted that, while we must trust the Holy Spirit for guidance, we should not presume upon Him, nor should we expect God to make up for our own laziness. Study, learning and teaching all had their place in God's economy and, while Christ gave to His church

3. For details see J.I. Packer, *Fundamentalism and the Word of God*, I.V.P. 1958, p. 103.

'pastors and teachers', they too needed teaching and training for the ministry that their God-given gifts should be used to the full.

Latimer may have lacked some of the discernment that Bilney possessed but he had more energy and eloquence. He was to be Tyndale's complement. What Tyndale was to do for England by his pen, Latimer was to do by his preaching. The zeal that he had formerly shown in saying mass was now reharnessed as he preached Christ crucified. He preached to the clergy in Latin and to the people in English. As a yeoman's son, he spoke the language that the merchants and peasants understood. He took homely illustrations from their everyday life to explain the passage of Scripture that he was expounding and, while at times his yeomanlike bluntness may have offended some of the sophisticated circle of courtiers before whom he later preached, these hearers needed the gospel as desperately as any.

'He was one of the first,' said an old historian, 'who in the days of King Henry VIII, set himself to preach the gospel in the truth and simplicity of it.' We must remember that the people had been starved of the gospel for centuries.

But how long would this preaching continue unopposed? Latimer remained above reproach in observance of formal religion, as did Bilney. They still accepted the mass and either attended or celebrated it regularly. Guesses might be made regarding the debates that took place in the White Horse, and the identity of the people who slipped in there might be noted by some watchful proctor, but there was nothing that could be openly attacked. In July 1525 the Bishop of Ely even granted Bilney a licence to preach anywhere in his diocese.

* * * * * * *

1525

However, Nicholas West, Bishop of Ely, had his spies and, probably acting on information received, one day at the end of 1525 he swooped without warning, as Latimer was preaching to members of the university. Obviously the bishop expected to catch him spreading heretical ideas and thus to obtain a watertight case against him.

Latimer showed himself to be a wise and bold diplomat. He stopped speaking and stood respectfully silent in the pulpit as the bishop and his episcopal train entered the church. When they were all seated, he announced that such important people demanded a new theme. He chose a text appropriate to the bishop and spoke on Hebrews 9:11: 'Christ being come, a High Priest of good things to come'. He then spoke of the duties and offices of all priests, and of bishops in particular, and of the life of Christ and the perfect pattern that He had set for all clergy. West, surprisingly enough, heard him out but he must have seethed as he listened, especially when Latimer, speaking generally, described the bishops of his day as being 'not of that race of bishops which Christ meant to have succeeded Him in His church, but rather of the fellowship of Caiaphas and Annas'.

It is not known what Latimer had been preaching on before West's appearance, but now the bishop had heard enough. He sent for Latimer after the sermon and thanked him for describing his duties in such detail. He then told Latimer that there was something he wanted him to do for him — preach a sermon against Martin Luther and his doctrine.

It was an ingenious trap but Latimer was more than a match for it. 'My lord, I am not acquainted with the doctrine of Luther, nor are we permitted here to read his works and therefore it were but a vain thing for me to refute his doctrine, not understanding what he hath written, nor what opinion he holdeth. Sure I am that I have preached before you this day no man's doctrine, but only the doctrine of God out of the Scriptures.'

The caution and shrewdness of Latimer's reply was too much for West. He lost his temper and said, 'Well, well, Mr Latimer, I perceive that you somewhat smell of the pan: you will repent this gear some day.'

Latimer's feelings must have been mixed as he watched the bishop depart, but he had stood firmly by what he believed and, as he had told the bishop, he did not preach any man's doctrine but only what he found in Scripture. He called for a return to the gospel way of life as known in the early church. He revolted against ritual and sacerdotalism and all the superstition that surrounded them. At that time he and his friends still did not question the central doctrine of the mass or the authority of the pope, on which the church of Rome stood or fell. But they exalted the authority of Scripture and, as they dug deeper into the Word, the teaching of the mass and the authority of the pope would both topple like a forest tree when the axe is laid at its roots.

West wasted no time. He denounced Latimer from the pulpit and formally suspended his licence to preach in his diocese or anywhere in the university. This appeared a catastrophe to Latimer and his friends. The most gifted preacher who had joined their ranks was silenced. What could Latimer do now, and who would be silenced next?

3. Trial by Wolsey

1525 — 1526

Prior Barnes's face darkened with anger as Latimer told them of the bishop's orders.

'A murrain on him! Who does he think he is? But we will show him. Master Latimer, come with me. I have a plan.'

Dr Robert Barnes, the Prior of the Augustinian Priory at Cambridge strode out of the White Horse tavern with Latimer. The small group gathered there looked at each other uneasily. Barnes's temper and impetuosity were well known among them. Since his conversion, Barnes had been welcomed into the fellowship of the White Horse, but soon after he came to a knowledge of the truth he began to show a zeal that was reckless at times.

Barnes was a Norfolk man, from Lynn, who came to Cambridge at an early age to enrol as a novice at the house of the Augustinian Friars. He then went to Louvain, where he was awarded his first Doctor of Divinity degree.[1] On his return to Cambridge he soon became prior of the house he had served as novice. His love of letters led him from the classics to Paul's Epistles. He still did not know the saving power of the gospel but he studied the Scriptures and lectured on them. He made quite a name for himself as a preacher and one of his contemporaries described him as 'one of a merry scoffing wit, friarlike, and as a good fellow in company was beloved by many'.

Thomas Bilney had been watching quietly and had seen the increased keenness that Barnes showed in the study and discussions on the teaching of the New Testament. He bided

1. In 1523 Barnes was awarded a second Doctor of Divinity degree at Cambridge.

his time and during 1525 Bilney and Barnes talked about the change of heart that was needed. We have no details, but it is recorded that through 'that good Master Bilney', Barnes was 'converted wholly unto Christ'.

Robert Barnes threw himself into the work with enthusiasm and joined the discussions at the White Horse inn with zeal. Soon after this came the startling news that Latimer was barred from all pulpits. Barnes was angered by this and, as his house was exempt from any rules or orders the bishop might make, he started planning.

Soon after this, on Sunday, Christmas Eve, 1525, the black-cowled company of the Augustinian Priory were surprised to see Hugh Latimer enter the pulpit in their chapel and take the service. Priors had long been the despair of bishops, and Robert Barnes was no exception. His house was responsible only to the pope and his cardinals — bishops could be ignored. So, despite the bishop's action, Barnes had opened his pulpit to Latimer.

Barnes, however, had no intention of leaving the matter there. He intended carrying the war into the bishop's camp. The same Sunday he preached from the pulpit of St Edward's, the chapel of Clare and Trinity Colleges. If Barnes could have restrained himself and preached the gospel, things might have been different. But he saw some of the strong opponents of the Reformers and also some personal enemies, and made many caustic comments. He attacked the bishops — they 'were followers of Judas'. Cardinal Wolsey, Archbishop of York and papal legate, came in for special attention. Wolsey, a lover of pomp and ceremony, was attacked for his rich clothes, his cushions, his golden shoes and his red gloves, which Barnes called 'bloody gloves to keep him warm amidst his ceremonies'.

A storm of protest arose after the service, and charges were brought against Barnes to the Vice-Chancellor of Cambridge University. An inquiry was held and the news was conveyed to Wolsey in London. Barnes insisted that he had been misunderstood and he offered to preach the next Sunday and clarify matters. The vice-chancellor had no intention of

letting him loose again and curtly declined. Barnes was forbidden to preach until the matter had been settled by
Cardinal Wolsey himself.

This divided the university. Many were opposed to the
Reformers, but Barnes had his friends. Much as Latimer and
Bilney regretted Barnes's behaviour, they could not abandon
him. As the White Horse fellowship had been growing, the
vice-chancellor had to watch his step and act cautiously.

In London, Wolsey was concerned. News had reached him
from the Continent that some daring Englishman (Tyndale)
had translated the New Testament into English, and was
about to flood England with this 'dangerous' book. For some
time rumours had reached him that at Cambridge books of a
Lutheran sort were filtering in from Germany. To Wolsey a
little heresy was permissible — with him it was an error — but
tilting at his person he would not permit. Barnes was arrested
and taken to London (February 1526) and brought
before Wolsey privately. Fortunately for those in Cambridge,
Dr Fairman of Queen's College heard of the plan to seize the
forbidden books and sent word to hide them. When the
sergeant-at-arms arrived and searched for the books he drew a
blank and the Christians at Cambridge breathed more freely.

Thomas Wolsey, the butcher's son from Ipswich who rose
to be the most powerful man in church and state, had started
off modestly. Under Henry VII he became royal chaplain,
but he did not wish to spend all his days saying mass. He
secured the king's favour and, under his son, Henry VIII,
became Bishop of Tournai (in Flanders), then Bishop of
Lincoln and Archbishop of York. Wolsey was not content;
he wanted to be Archbishop of Canterbury. To conciliate
him, he was created cardinal in 1515. Wolsey wanted secular
greatness, too, and he was only satisfied when he became
Lord Chancellor of England. The king left much of the affairs
of state in Wolsey's hands and spent his time in sport and the
pleasures of court life.

When the pope appointed Wolsey legate in 1518, thus
placing all colleges, monasteries, bishops and spiritual courts
under his rule, Wolsey felt compensated for the loss of

Canterbury. His vanity knew no bounds. While Barnes's
attack was indiscreet, it was fully justified. When Wolsey
appeared in public, two priests carried two huge silver crosses
before him: one to mark his dignity as papal legate, the other
his dignity as archbishop. He built Hampton Court as his
residence and had a staff of more than five hundred. He wore
a dress of scarlet velvet and silk, and his shoes were em-
broidered with gold and silver.

Wolsey looked haughtily at this prior who had dared to
preach against him. Gardiner, the cardinal's secretary, had
been Barnes's tutor at Cambridge, and when he and Edward
Foxe, also a Cambridge man, brought Barnes in, they pleaded
with Wolsey to be merciful to him. The cardinal read the
articles of accusation sent from Cambridge, and Barnes
sought to defend himself. Wolsey may have been inclined to
wink at a little heresy, but he criticized Barnes for his attack
on his person. Quite justifiably he said that it was 'a sermon
more fit to be preached on a stage than in a pulpit'.

Barnes was urged to submit to Wolsey and acknowledge his
heresy but he refused and the next day, together with several
German Lutherans, he was brought for trial before the
Bishops of London, Rochester, Bath and St Asaph's. He again
refused to admit his heresy and was committed to the Fleet
prison.

Poor Barnes was now in the grip of a relentless machine,
and his learning was of little use. Time after time he was con-
fronted with the terrible words: 'Abjure or burn!' Eventually
he recanted and, with the Germans, was brought to St Paul's,
where the Bishop of Rochester preached against Luther.
Barnes was subjected to the penance of the convicted heretic
— carrying a faggot three times round the fire where Protestant books were burning, and then throwing the faggot into
the fire. The faggot was a solemn warning that if he lapsed
into heresy again it would not be a faggot that would be
thrust into the fire, but he would be fastened to a stake and
burned himself. After kneeling and craving forgiveness from
'Mother Church,' Barnes was absolved and received back into
the church. He was then returned to the Fleet prison. Later

he was sent to the house of the Austin Friars in London and eventually escaped overseas.

The heresy hunt was on in earnest now. Cambridge came under the full floodlight of Wolsey's searching gaze. If Cambridge had been hiding a heretic like Barnes, how many others might be sheltering in her colleges and cloisters? He gave orders that a thorough examination should take place.

Latimer and Bilney had their enemies, too. Those who reject the gospel often have no love for the preachers of the truth. Several people made accusations against Latimer and he was summoned before Wolsey. Circumstances had changed since Barnes came before the cardinal. Wolsey had had his revenge on the man who had dared to insult his person; his foreign policy had proved successful and he was in a much better mood. As he lounged back on the gold cushions clad in his scarlet robes and questioned Latimer, he was struck by the latter's manliness, his frankness and bold demeanour.

Wolsey soon found that Latimer was not infected by the 'Lutheran heresy', as he told him he had not read any of Luther's works, but pointed out that he had studied 'the ancient doctors of the church and also the school-doctors'. On hearing this, Wolsey ordered that Latimer should answer questions put to him by his two chaplains. As Latimer was still thoroughly up-to-date in his studies, he answered them clearly and even corrected their misquotations in places.

Wolsey was mystified as to why Latimer had been falsely accused and sent to him. Then Latimer told him of the Bishop of Ely's visit to the church, and of his sermon on the duties and offices of a bishop, tactfully omitting to mention his sudden change of theme.

The cardinal was now completely satisfied regarding his orthodoxy and learning. 'Did you not preach any other doctrine than you have rehearsed?' he asked.

'No, surely,' Latimer replied.

'If the Bishop of Ely cannot abide such doctrine as you have here repeated, you shall have my licence, and shall preach it unto his beard, let him say what he will,' Wolsey declared.

When Latimer returned to Cambridge he had in his pocket Wolsey's licence to preach, not just in Cambridge but anywhere in England. He promptly resumed preaching at Cambridge. He had no idea of the stormy seas he would soon be sailing. All seemed to be going smoothly now that Wolsey had given him his licence.

In the spring of 1526, unknown to both Wolsey and Latimer, an unsuspected ally had silently reached England's shores. Borne by merchants and carefully concealed among their cargo, the first copies of Tyndale's New Testament had been brought to England by ships from Antwerp. After the consignment reached London it was quietly distributed throughout the country. Very soon, in shops and cottages, in parsonages and even monastery cells, the Word of God, given to the learned by Erasmus a decade before, was being read and studied by the ordinary people. The clarity of the language, in plain English, struck the readers forcibly and prepared the hearts of many for the preaching of the Word by Latimer and his colleagues.

*   *   *   *   *   *   *

In the history of the church there is a constant interweaving of political with religious matters as God, in His sovereignty, uses kings and rulers to execute His purpose. As Latimer returned with Wolsey's licence in his pocket. Henry VIII was becoming increasingly attracted to Anne Boleyn. When this young woman, destined to become Queen of England, was maid-of-honour at the French court she had already learned something of the gospel through Margaret of Valois — sister of Francis I, King of France.

Despite numerous attempts to blacken the character of Anne Boleyn, history shows that, while she was undoubtedly ambitious, she was above all things honest and determined at this point to preserve her virginity until she was married to the man who sought her hand. She would not become a royal mistress; for her it was marriage or nothing. Foiled by Wolsey from marrying young Lord Percy, whom she loved dearly, she hated the cardinal from that day, but was content to remain single until she met another suitor.

If Anne was ambitious, Wolsey was a hundred times more so. Since 1518 he had coveted the papal diadem. When Pope Adrian VI died in 1523, he thought it was within his grasp. His fury knew no bounds when Clement VII was created the new pope — had not the Emperor Charles V promised it to him? Wisely he concealed his anger from Henry.

'Wolsey as pope would, humanly speaking, have tightened the cords which already bound England so closely to Rome; but Wolsey, rejected, could hardly fail to throw himself into tortuous paths which would perhaps contribute to the emancipation of the church,' says D'Aubigné. About this time, Queen Catherine reproached Wolsey for his dissolute life. Charles had foiled his attempt for the tiara; he would have his revenge on both of them.

It is ironic that Wolsey, to get revenge on Charles through his aunt, Catherine of Aragon, should suggest to Henry a divorce from Catherine. They had been married nearly twenty years but the king already had doubts about the legitimacy of his marriage because Catherine had borne him no son.

To achieve this revenge, Wolsey wove such a tangled web that he hardly knew where the end of the thread lay. He suggested that Margaret of Valois would be a suitable bride for Henry. The cardinal never dreamed that the king's desire for a divorce would be accentuated by his passion for Anne Boleyn, or that when Henry eventually succeeded, it would be to marry a friend of the Reformers!

'It was not the king's passion for Anne Boleyn. . . but the passion of a cardinal for the triple crown,' which set in motion the wheels that led to England's emancipation from Rome.

4. Cambridge ministry

1527 – 1529

Hugh Latimer rose from his desk and walked over to the window. He looked out of the small panes towards King's College Chapel which towered majestically above the other buildings. His mind went back to the time when he believed that the only place he could draw near to God was in church or chapel. Now that he had come to know Christ, since that day when Bilney came to him, all was changed and he realized that he could draw near to God anywhere. Latimer still loved to worship in church, but his heart went out to those around him. Their eyes were still blinded to the fact that if they came to Christ, they, too, could draw closer to God than the priest conducting the service.

Much had happened since last year when he had returned from London with Wolsey's licence in his pocket. For Latimer it had been a period of quiet activity and steady progress, with a few skirmishes with priests who hated evangelical doctrine. It had matured his faith, he had grown spiritually, and his conviction of the need for better biblical teaching for the ignorant people had been deepened. In his preaching work Latimer became increasingly aware of the need for the Bible in the English language. How could you teach people effectively if no copy of the Bible was available to them?

News of the spread of Tyndale's translation throughout England reached him from time to time, but it was still a forbidden book. Many people had been imprisoned for even possessing a copy, and Tyndale himself led a hunted existence on the Continent, moving from place to place so that no one knew exactly where he was.

A slow smile spread across Latimer's face as he thought of

one of the blunders made by Tyndale's persecutors. In May of that year Archbishop Warham, fired with zeal to prevent England from reading the Bible, had suggested a naive plan to get hold of all the copies by starting a 'book fund' to which the bishops subscribed. With the sixty-two pounds nine shillings and fourpence collected they had bought up many New Testaments. This had helped Tyndale greatly, as finances were low, and another edition was speedily run through the press. It was ironic that Tyndale's worst enemy should have become his 'financier'.

Thanks to Wolsey's licence, Latimer had continued preaching without further interference from the Bishop of Ely. Although he did not realize it, the past year had widened his horizon in preaching and he was digging deeper into the Word of God as he taught. He was more conscious of the need for free inquiry and private judgement — both forbidden by the church. His popularity with students grew. Sometimes there were more than the church could hold, and they hung on his words.

'When Master Stafford read, and Master Latimer preached, then was Cambridge blessed.' This had become a local proverb at Cambridge.

'Oh, how vehement was he in rebuking all sins, namely idolatry, false and idle swearing, covetousness and whoredom; again, how sweet and pleasant were his words in exhorting unto virtue!' said Thomas Becon, later one of Cranmer's chaplains. 'He spake nothing but it left as it were certain pricks or stings in the hearts of the hearers, which moved them to consent to his doctrine.'

'I have an ear for other preachers,' said Sir John Cheke, later tutor to Edward VI, 'but I have a heart for Latimer.'

Obviously such preaching was not going to pass without opposition and though he was protected by Wolsey's licence from actual imprisonment or bodily harm, his enemies arraigned him verbally and abused him. But Latimer knew that Martin Luther had been attacked in the same way in Germany, and as he studied his New Testament he learned that his Lord and Master, too, had suffered from the leaders of the Jewish church. He could not expect immunity.

Latimer's face darkened as he turned and looked towards Great St Mary's, the university church. It was after he had preached there that Bilney had come to him. Now Bilney was in deep trouble. Earlier in the year, with a friend named Thomas Arthur, he had gone on a preaching campaign, mainly in Suffolk and Norfolk. Bilney had not only preached the gospel, but had attacked the superstitious practices of worshipping crucifixes and relics. When he came near London he had been arrested and imprisoned. Latimer felt keenly for him. Theirs had been such a David and Jonathan relationship. How was Bilney getting on?

* * * * * * *

1527

The grey stone arches and walls of the Chapter House in Westminster matched the November weather. There was a liberal sprinkling of autumn colours, too, in the scarlet and gold robes of the clergy and purple worn by the bishops, but the centre of the stage was taken by Wolsey with his golden cushions and scarlet clothes. By contrast, the prisoner Thomas Bilney seemed small and insignificant as he stood before them in his sombre clothes. Wolsey's face was hard as he stared at him. Much had happened since Latimer and Bilney had come before him the previous year and he was becoming tougher with heretics.

One of the witnesses called on behalf of Bilney had revealed that his curate, Thomas Garret, had been selling New Testaments and other heretical books to the students at Oxford. Wolsey had founded Cardinal College only two years previously and named it after himself in his usual vain fashion, and he desired above all else that it should be free from heresy. He did not want another Wycliffe to arise. Now it appeared that this college was as tainted as the others, and he was already investigating the matter. Bilney was not going to get off so easily this time.

The prisoner faced a string of questions from Wolsey and the bishops. Witnesses abounded, especially friars, because Bilney preached against images and they could see a fruitful source of income in danger. Day after day the trial dragged on and Bilney faced a continual barrage of questions. Was prayer to be addressed to Christ alone? Did he believe that all Christians, laity as well as clergy, were priests who could bind and loose as if they had the Holy Spirit? Ought the English language to be used for mass? Did he believe that the Bible should be translated into English and read to the common people at divine service?

Under this assault Bilney stood firm for a while. Three times, under pressure from Tunstall, Bishop of London, he was exhorted to recant and place himself at the mercy of the church. On the great question of mass Bilney had proved orthodox. He did not doubt that the wafer and wine became the real body and blood of our Lord when the priest spoke the words at mass. The Roman church called this 'transubstantiation'. Bilney and Latimer had not changed their views on this and Bilney accepted the authority of the church. But he faced a ruthless machine that had held power over the lives of men for over a thousand years — and not only their lives but also their souls, since the church claimed to be able to close the doors of heaven to any whom she declared a heretic. One writer has said, 'Columbus was not doing so brave a thing in confronting the unknown West as Bilney was attempting, facing an eternal voyage with no blessing of the church upon him.'

In December, Tunstall pleaded three times with Bilney to recant. He recognized his sincerity and orthodoxy on most points. Bilney asked for time to consult with his friends. Apart from Latimer, all advised him to recant. He then broke down and yielded but afterwards, like Peter, became the most miserable of men.

He was condemned to prison for a year and made to walk bareheaded round St Paul's carrying a faggot on his shoulder. This was a warning that if he came up for trial again it would be death by fire for him. He was then cast into the Tower of

London. When he was released a year later, he returned to
Cambridge a broken-hearted man. Latimer and other friends
gathered round and sought to comfort him. He knew he had
saved his body, but inwardly he was tormented. Latimer
never forgot this. Years later, in a sermon preached before
Edward VI, he said, 'I knew a man myself, Bilney, little
Bilney, that blessed martyr of God, what time he had borne
his faggot, and was come again to Cambridge, had such
conflicts within himself. . . . Here is a good lesson for you, my
friends; if ever you come in danger, in durance, in prison for
God's quarrel, and for His sake, as he did. . . I will advise
first, and above all things, to abjure all your friends, all your
friendships. . . . It is they that shall undo you, and not your
enemies.'[1]

Yet those friends did much to help Bilney at this time, and
in the coming years they learned to cast off that fear of man
which brings a snare and stood firmly before judges without
denying their faith.

* * * * * * *

While this had been taking place in London, the gospel had
continued to spread in towns and villages throughout
England. The prelates and cardinals might burn the New
Testament when they could and persecute those who read it,
but when there is a real hunger in the hearts of men for the
divine truth, the Word of God has its own way of spreading.
England was experiencing revival.

At this time John Tyball, who lived in Bumpstead, Essex,
was reading 1 Corinthians and came to the words: 'Eat of this
bread,' and 'Drink of this cup.' As he meditated on the
passage, he became convinced that what the church taught
about transubstantiation when the priest spoke the words at
mass was nothing but rubbish. 'Christ is present in the
Eucharist,' said Tyball, 'but He is there only for him that
believeth, and by a spiritual presence and action only.'

1. *Latimer's Sermons*, Parker Society, p. 222.

Clearly, laymen like Tyball were making faster progress in understanding spiritual things than Latimer and Bilney who had been saturated in the church's teachings.

While Tyndale was labouring overseas on his work of translation of the New Testament, others had caught the vision that inspired him. Miles Coverdale, who had trained under the unfortunate Barnes, had turned to the Scriptures and realized, as had Tyndale, that here was the only effective remedy for the maladies of the church.

'Wherever the Scripture is known it reformeth all things, and setteth everything in order. And why? Because it is given by the inspiration of God,' said Coverdale. He then felt burdened to undertake the same task that Tyndale had begun. The Bible meant so much to these two men that Coverdale felt it was good that two translations should be in progress at the same time. If Tyndale was caught and his work stopped, then Coverdale could continue. There was no sense of rivalry between them. In fact soon afterwards, in 1529, the two men met in Germany and worked together for a while. Coverdale was less skilled in languages than Tyndale, but he encouraged the exile in his work. Later, for various reasons, the two Reformers parted having decided it was better that each should continue the translation work separately.

During this time, Henry continued his efforts to gain a divorce from Catherine of Aragon. Anne Boleyn, to whom Henry had become more and more attracted, was ambitious and imprudent in some ways, yet she was feeling and generous. As the conflict with the church regarding a divorce from Catherine progressed, Anne decided to abandon the court in favour of the quiet Gothic halls of Hever Castle where she had grown up. She felt unable to look the unfortunate Catherine in the face. While Anne was ambitious for the throne, she had a great respect for Catherine. This young woman, who had much beauty, with black hair, oval face and dark eyes, had a graceful carriage, with much skill in dancing and great dignity. Her lovable character won many hearts among the people. Obviously, the older woman, Catherine,

Catherine of Aragon. *(Reproduced by courtesy of the National Portrait Gallery.)*

Anne Boleyn *(Reproduced by courtesy of the National Portrait Gallery.)*

with her Spanish features prematurely aged by her ascetic life, could not compete with Anne.

Nevertheless Anne suffered great mental conflict. Alone at Hever she had time to think what she would face if and when she gained the throne. She knew that Wolsey would ruin her if he could and she had other powerful enemies among the nobles. She lacked the piety of Margaret of Valois, but she sought the light and the truth and had a horror of superstition. When alone at Hever she did much reading. One day she opened a book called *The Obedience of a Christian Man*. It had been written by William Tyndale, smuggled into England and left at Hever by a friend of the Reformation.

'If thou believe the promises, then God's truth justifieth thee; that is, forgiveth thy sins and sealeth thee with His Holy Spirit.' Anne was gripped by this. 'If thou have true faith, so seest thou the exceeding and infinite love and mercy which God hath shown thee freely in Christ. . . .'

Tyndale's words did not change Anne's heart, but she marked the passages that impressed her most. The seeds of the Protestant doctrine, or rather the biblical doctrine, had been sown in her heart. She knew that Wolsey was hunting Tyndale and this gave her an affinity with him. Wolsey was their common enemy.

'The king's cause', as Foxe calls Henry's desire for a divorce, had started several years before. In 1526, the French ambassadors cast doubts on the validity of his marriage and therefore on the legitimacy of his daughter Mary. This brought the succession to the throne into dispute and menaced England with another civil war.

As one writer, Demaus, says, 'Some consider Henry as a profligate wretch. . . they believe that there never was any other reason for the divorce except the passion of a dissolute king for a younger and fairer woman than his wife. This theory is a very simple one, and certainly Henry's greatest admirers must admit that his relations with his numerous queens stand considerably in need of explanation and defence; still there are other facts concerning the divorce of which history is bound to take cognizance. It is certain, for example, that up to this period Henry's life had not been one of profligacy; he had not been blameless, indeed, but the theory which represents him as a lawless debauchee had very little confirmation in fact.'

If he had not previously questioned the legitimacy of his marriage, it is reasonable to suppose, now that the matter had been drawn to his attention, that Henry would ask whether his marriage was in fact condemned by God. Did Scripture condemn him? Leviticus said, 'They shall be childless.' This curse seemed to rest on Henry's house. Mary alone had survived out of the many children Catherine had borne him.

It was Catherine who always affirmed that Wolsey's desire for revenge upon the emperor had led him to suggest to Henry that his marriage was sinful, and so injure Charles through his aunt.[2]

It may seem irrelevant to spend time considering Henry's divorce, yet more was at stake than a king's passion for a woman. This desire was, under God, to play a vital part in shaping England's history. More important to us, it was to decide how much freedom Latimer and our other Reformers would have in preaching the gospel and reforming the church.

Even if Anne Boleyn had not attracted Henry, it seems probable that the question of divorce would have arisen and he would have sought the hand of another younger, fairer woman. Catherine was considerably older than Henry, her ascetic life had robbed her of her beauty and she was dull and morbid. Henry needed the company of a young and bright woman.

Just at that time Anne appeared on the scene. Much of her early history is obscure, but it is clear that Henry had seen her some years before and had admired her from a distance. Now, with a divorce apparently on its way, it was natural that he should turn to her. Henry thought the divorce would come quickly. It required the papal sanction, so he submitted

2. There are several schools of thought on this question but the author inclines to the view of those historians who regard Wolsey as the insti--gator of the divorce.

through his ambassadors the question of the lawfulness of his marriage with detailed and reasoned arguments. These, he was confident, would soon release him from wedlock and leave him free to choose a bride. Unfortunately, Henry's timing was wrong. Pope Clement VI was at the mercy of the emperor, Catherine's nephew, and Rome had been taken and sacked by his troops in May 1529.

The pope tried in vain to avoid offending either monarch and by cunning and diplomacy sought to postpone any definite decision. Time, he hoped, would cool Henry's passion. Catherine could enter a convent – but she refused. Henry, suggested Clement, might be allowed by the church to have two wives.

All these proposals were coldly swept aside by Henry. For him it was Anne or nobody. As time dragged on, he grew indignant at the way he was being treated. Had he not written *The Assertion of the Seven Sacraments* and been given the title 'Defender of the Faith'? These proved he was a good son of the church. England, too, had become indignant at this insult to her national independence.

Wolsey sensed his master's growing anger and urged Clement to make a decision. The result was that two papal legates were appointed to settle the matter. The pope appointed Cardinal Campeggio to sit with Wolsey and try the case in England. But while Campeggio was appointed in April 1528, it was not until June 1529 that he actually sat at the Great Hall of the Blackfriars, in London, to hear the case. He had been instructed by Clement to do everything possible to delay his journey and impede the trial. 'Advance slowly and never finish,' said Clement. Campeggio obeyed his orders carefully and the trial was a complete farce.

Catherine comported herself with true regal dignity. When she appeared in the Hall before the cardinals, she stepped forward and said firmly, 'I protest against the legates as incompetent judges, and appeal to the pope.' She knew she would get no justice when Wolsey was one of the judges, and refused to enter the court again.

After hearing both sides of the case, which dragged on into

late July, Campeggio adjourned the court on a ridiculous pre-
text and it never met again. Henry was furious. 'Either the
papacy pronounces my divorce from Catherine or I shall
divorce myself from the papacy,' he had said. But now he
was silent, partly from shock.

Wolsey was a broken man. When Campeggio left England
in the autumn of 1529, Wolsey was indicted for procuring
bulls from Rome and so breaking the Statute of Provisors. He
knew it was useless to plead that the king had authorized him
to do so. He admitted his guilt, resigned his office as
chancellor, asked for mercy and surrendered all his treasures,
including the palace of Hampton Court.

The cardinal was permitted to go to York which he had
never visited although he had been Archbishop of York since
1514. He left for York in early 1530 and intended to enter
the city with his usual pomp, but was arrested before he
reached there by Lord Percy, whose affection for Anne
Boleyn had been thwarted by Wolsey some years previously.
Wolsey was charged with treason but while on his journey
back to London for trial he died at Leicester Abbey on 29
November 1530.

Since Wolsey's fall Sir Thomas More had been appointed
Chancellor of England, the first layman to hold the office
since 1386. He summoned a Parliament for November 1529,
the first for more than six years. More has been portrayed by
some as a compassionate man with much feeling, but this is
only one facet of his make-up. His love was limited to his
family and close friends, such as Erasmus. All were staunch
Catholics. When it came to those who veered from the teachings of the church and became heretics, More was ruthless.
The stake had been idle for too long in his opinion. 'Recant
or burn,' was More's motto. How would the Reformers fare
with such a man as chancellor?

5. King's preacher

1529 — 1531

Latimer was grave-faced when news reached Cambridge of Sir Thomas More's accession to the office of chancellor. More had been deliberately chosen by Henry. The king's contest with Rome had filled the Reformers with hope. The humble people who lived near the sea were reading Tyndale's New Testament and Luther's writings. The clergy were filled with concern and wanted this stopped. Henry, however, was on bad terms with them. He needed someone as mediator between himself and the clergy, and Sir Thomas More met his need.

In his earlier days, More had been a keen humanist, a friend of John Colet, who had begun lectures on St Paul's letters over thirty years previously. Now he was turning into an inquisitor. His noble understanding, that had enabled him to write *Utopia*, was passing from ascetic practices to fanaticism. Colet had persuaded him not to enter a monastery, but More wore a hair shirt next to his skin until the day he died.

Earlier in the year (1529), Bilney had returned to Cambridge and at first had appeared inconsolable. By degrees Latimer had been able to encourage him to take up some of his former duties and the two friends were to be seen walking on 'Heretics' Hill' deep in conversation.

Since the fall of Wolsey, some had cast aspersions on the validity of the licence by which Latimer preached. Since Wolsey had fallen they claimed that it was no longer valid, but Latimer shrewdly pointed out to them that it was only Wolsey the statesman who had fallen. He was still cardinal and papal legate, therefore his licence was as valid as ever. Latimer would not stop preaching because of the unhappy prelate's fall.

In December he preached two sermons called the 'Sermons on the Card'. This filled the university with strife and debate. It was then customary to celebrate Christmas by playing cards. Latimer seized on this as a way of capturing his hearers' imagination and he showed how they could play Christ's cards. One important card, he said, was connected with our Lord's words: 'When thou makest thine oblation at mine altar, and there dost remember that thy neighbour hath anything against thee, lay down there thy oblation, and go first and reconcile thy neighbour, and then come and offer thy oblation.'[1] This card was often misplayed; men provoked and injured one another but forgot that God wanted them to bring back their neighbours in love before coming to worship Him.

As Latimer looked at the worship offered to God, he saw nothing but a constant breaking of this rule of Christ. Sacrifice was substituted for obedience and the church taught her children to violate God's laws in order to obey hers. This grieved Latimer's heart and made him earnestly exhort his congregation to obey Christ's teaching: 'If you will build a glorious church unto God, see first yourselves to be in charity with your neighbours, and suffer not them to be offended by your works. Then, when ye come into your parish church, you bring with you the holy temple of God. Again, if you list to gild and paint Christ in your churches, and honour Him in vestments, see that before your eyes the poor people die not for lack of meat, drink and clothing. Then do you deck the very true temple of God, and honour Him in rich vestures that will never be worn, and so forth use yourselves, according to the commandments. . . .'[2]

This appears clear teaching from Scripture. It was not doctrinally controversial, as were some of the sermons preached by the Continental Reformers, yet it aroused a storm of controversy. Latimer's opponents knew that his homely sermons took the public fancy and many came to

1. *Latimer's Sermons*, page 8.
2. *Latimer's Sermons*, page 8.

hear him preach. He had put forth his hand to touch the sacred edifice of the church and, furthermore, he had suggested that money should be given to the poor rather than to the church. To cut off their offerings was to stem the flow of money for the clergy and this must be resisted.

Buckenham, Prior of the Dominican friars, was chosen as champion of the old orthodoxy and preached against Latimer, who had implied in most of his sermons that all should have the freedom to read the Bible. This, said Buckenham, would be very dangerous to the layman, because it was full of figurative language which the ordinary man would misunderstand to his own ruin.

'Where Scripture saith, "No man that layeth his hand to the plough, and looketh back, is meet for the kingdom of God," will not the ploughman, when he readeth these words, be apt forthwith to cease from his plough, and then where will be the sowing and harvest?' asked Buckenham. 'And so, also, when the simple man reads the words, "If thine eye offend thee, pluck it out, and cast it from thee," incontinent he will pluck out his eyes, and so the whole realm will be full of blind men, to the great decay of the nation.'

Latimer's ready wit seized on this with delight. 'The ploughmen and simple men can be safely trusted,' he declared in his next sermon, with Prior Buckenham sitting in the centre of the congregation. 'Every speech hath its metaphors, so common and vulgar to all men, that the very painters do paint them on walls and in houses. As, for example, . . . ' and here Latimer looked straight at Buckenham, 'when they paint a fox preaching out of a friar's cowl, none is so mad as to take this to be a fox that preacheth, but know well enough the meaning of the matter, which is to point out unto us what hypocrisy, craft and subtle dissimulation lieth hid many times in these friars' cowls, willing us to beware of them.'

The prior was surrounded by guffaws of laughter and he beat a hasty retreat from the church. Latimer was enjoying himself and other opponents fared as badly. They were no match for his keen wit. The controversy grew hotter and St

John's College contained a number of men who were bitterly opposed to Latimer and all Reformation teaching. When Latimer prepared this sermon, he little dreamed that it was to cause as great a controversy at Cambridge as Luther caused in Germany when he nailed the ninety-five theses to the church door at Wittenburg.

Cambridge was only a small town in the sixteenth century and the quarrel soon came to the ears of the vice-chancellor. In January 1530 he ordered both parties to appear before the senate and ordered them to stop their dispute and to refrain from starting any fresh ones. If they disobeyed the king would be angry, as he had heard all about the unrest. Latimer was ordered, under threat of excommunication, 'to touch no such things in the pulpit as had been in controversy between him and others'. [3] Apart from this, he was warned to be careful in his sermons and to avoid offence to others. His opponents of St John's College were told that he had given an adequate explanation of the matters that he had been charged with so they, likewise, were to be silent.

Peace was restored but Dr Buckmaster, the vice-chancellor, was concerned with more than the peace of the university he wanted to please the king. He had received a letter from the royal almoner in which he stated, 'It hath been greatly complained unto the king's highness of the shameful contentions. . . between Mr Latimer and certain of St John's College. . . . It is not unlikely but that they of St John's proceedeth of some private malice towards Mr Latimer, and that also they be animated so to do by their master, Mr Watson, and such other my Lord of Rochester's friends. Which malice also, peradventure, cometh partly for that Mr Latimer favoureth the king's cause; and I assure you it is so reported unto the king.' [4]

The 'king's cause' continued to bring dissension throughout England. But the letter makes it clear Henry had heard

3. Lamb, *Original Documents*, Corpus Christi College, Cambridge, p. 16.
4. Lamb, *Original Documents*, p. 14.

that Latimer was one of those who favoured his case and, while he wanted no controversy at Cambridge, neither did he wish an eloquent man who favoured him to be silenced by the clergy. Henry had an eye to the future and he could not tell when he might need Latimer.

The previous autumn Henry, after his disappointment with Wolsey and Campeggio, had found the man who had come up with a fresh idea. In the autumn of 1529 Henry had left London to avoid the plague that had settled on the city, and two of his attendants, when staying at Waltham, had met Thomas Cranmer who had been told of the king's problem.

Thomas Cranmer was a fellow of Jesus' College, Cambridge, and he had dug deeply into the Scriptures. He had been troubled by Luther's first book and had said, 'I must know on which side the truth lies. There is only one infallible source, the Scriptures.' He had then spent three years studying the Bible without using any commentary or book of theology. Eventually his eyes were opened and he saw God's plan of salvation. Cranmer had been lecturing at Cambridge for some time and his favourite saying to those who complained that the Scriptures were hard to understand was: 'Explain the obscure passages by those which are clear, Scripture by Scripture. Seek, pray, and He who has the key of David will open them to you.'

Fox and Gardiner, the king's attendants, sat with Cranmer and discussed the king's problem. Cranmer had given much thought to this matter already. 'You are not in the right path, you should not cling to the decisions of the church. The true question is this,' Cranmer said, 'What says the Word of God? When God has spoken man must obey.' 'But how shall we know what God has said?' asked Fox and Gardiner. 'Consult the universities,' Cranmer replied. 'They will discern it more surely than Rome.'

This was a new idea to both Henry and his followers. The question had been put to the universities before but then the king had just wanted them to give their own opinions. This was a different way of approaching it. Now the question was: 'What does God say in His Word?' They were, in fact, grasp-

Henry VIII. *(Reproduced by courtesy of the National Portrait Gallery.)*

Thomas Cranmer. *(Reproduced by courtesy of the National Portrait Gallery.)*

ing the principle that underlay the whole Reformation – the Word of God is above the church. If this principle had been constantly held by all the Reformers and they had been given freedom to practise it without interference from king or state, the Reformation in England might have taken a very different course. 'The church says,' was the standard answer given by prince and peasant to every question of a religious nature. For centuries, during the Dark Ages, the church had been steadily elevating herself until she was not merely equal to Scripture but far superior to it. The fact that this was a gradual process is a timely warning for today. The ecumenical movement has taken up many of the characteristics of the medieval church.

* * * * * * *

When the news was brought to Henry, he exclaimed, 'Cranmer has the right sow by the ear!' Dr Cranmer was appointed one of the royal chaplains and the king brought the question to Oxford and Cambridge, and to the main foreign universities. So, in February 1530, soon after the dispute about the 'Sermons on the Card' had died down, the vice-chancellor had to submit to the university the question whether the law of God forbad marriage with a deceased brother's wife. This resulted in a committee which included Latimer, as well as several who were bitter opponents of the Reformation. Fox and Gardiner were sent to Cambridge to get a decision in Henry's favour. After much arguing, Gardiner succeeded but when he made his report to the king he made no reference to Latimer. As Gardiner was strongly opposed to the Reformers this was probably intentional. Fortunately, Sir William Butts, the royal physician, was at Cambridge during the debate and on his return he told Henry of Latimer's ability. The result was that he was invited to Windsor to preach before the king during Lent.

The fame of Latimer's preaching having reached the ears of the king, Henry now wanted to judge for himself what this man was like. If he could cause such a sensation at Cambridge, he was no ordinary preacher. On 13 March 1530, he preached before the king and the court for the first time but unfortunately the subject of his sermon has not been recorded. We do know, however, that Latimer always framed his doctrine according to his audience so there was no collection of soft, flattering words but rather a plain, honest exposition of the duties of kings and all in authority. The Vice-Chancellor of Cambridge had arrived with his university's decision on Henry's question and he records that when speaking with the king 'by and by he greatly praised Mr Latimer's sermon'.[5] Latimer's star was rising.

Hugh Latimer continued to preach at court throughout Lent and this was his entrance to that wider sphere where he was destined to exercise his ministry. He may on this occasion have met Anne Boleyn for the first time. She always had a high regard for him and his teaching. As he had done much by favouring the 'king's cause' in his preaching, Anne had good reason to be grateful to this honest and outspoken preacher who always put God first in his thoughts and actions and did not cringe before the king. For his services that Lent, Latimer was paid five pounds, a large sum in those days, and it certainly indicated that he was an outstanding preacher in Henry's eyes.

Soon after his return to Cambridge, Latimer again found that he was pulled out of his obscurity. The vice-chancellor had received another letter from the king. Henry wanted the best learned men in divinity to form a commission to examine the many religious books that were circulating in England, to select those that were 'good and fruitful' — all others would be banned. Twelve Cambridge men and twelve Oxford men were to form the main body of the commission. Latimer was one of the first to be chosen. As the commission had fanatical enemies of the Reformation on it, men like Sir Thomas More, Gardiner and Tunstall, things were going to be difficult for Latimer and his friends. It is interesting that one of the people who sat with Hugh Latimer was the famous

5. Lamb, *Original Documents.*

scholar William Latimer, who was unrelated to Hugh but a true friend of the Reformation.

The commission sat for twelve days from the middle of May 1530 and finished on 24 May. The debate had been vehement and much skill and learning had been shown by those on both sides. 'Christ's sheep hear no man's voice but Christ's,' said Latimer when he was ordered to submit to the church. He could see clearly that the church had set up its voice in place of Christ's, but no Reformer could agree to this. The people must have the Bible to read for themselves to hear the voice of Christ.

Unfortunately Latimer and his friends were completely outnumbered. Tyndale's works were condemned as 'full of great errors and pestilent heresies', his New Testament translation and also the Pentateuch, which was now complete, were both heavily censured and their use banned. What must have seemed the crowning insult to Latimer was the fact that his name was 'appended' with the others of the commission to a proclamation that he had opposed and which he hated with all his heart. He knew that the English people must have the New Testament and Tyndale had provided it. The only gleam of hope for Latimer and his friends was the promise made by Henry that he would have a translation made for the English people 'when he saw their manner and behaviour convenient to receive the same'. Was this an honest promise and would the king keep it? This doubt must have gnawed at Latimer's mind.

At least one writer has accused Latimer of weakness when on this commission and believes that he gave way in the end. But as Demaus points out, Latimer's name was 'appended', that is, added on to the list of signatories, doubtless to give the king the impression that none of them had dared to disagree with him. Latimer, however, did disagree and was prepared to stand alone.[6]

All seemed to be favouring Rome, and Tunstall, Bishop of

6 A similar case to this occurred when Henry was before Campeggio and Wolsey. The Bishop of Rochester's name was appended, without his

London, celebrated this by bringing out the Testaments that
he had bought and kept under lock and key, and burning
them publicly at St Paul's. People watched the bonfire and
many shook their heads. 'Since the priests destroy the
Scriptures, their teaching must contradict what God has said
or why do they fear them?' they asked.

True to type, Latimer did not let matters rest there. After
much thought, he sat down and wrote a letter to Henry later
that year in which he asked that there might be free circulation of the Holy Scriptures in English. Henry made a
promise and however vague it was, Latimer grasped it firmly
since it was the only hope for England. Together with the
other Reformers, he knew that there could be no reform or
progress unless the Word of God had free course. His one
hope was that Henry's conscience would be stirred. It was a
noble letter and a bold one. Latimer knew full well that
people who addressed Henry boldly normally had a short life
but that did not deter him.

The letter is too long to quote in full but this portion gives
us a good idea of what it was like. 'You have promised us the
Word of God, perform your promise now rather than tomorrow,' Latimer wrote. 'God will have the faith defended,
not by man or man's power, but by His Word only, by the
which He hath evermore defended it, and that by a way far
above man's power or reason, as all the stories of the Bible
make mention. . . . The day is at hand when you shall give an
account of your office, and of the blood that hath been shed
with your sword.'[7] Latimer risked his life by using this
language but he was prepared for death if need be.

Strange to say, Henry took no action against Latimer.
Some part of Henry's character responded to such courage.
He was not a coward himself and he admired bravery in

consent to a document drawn up by the other bishops. (See J. H. Merle
D'Aubigné, *The Reformation in England*, Banner of Truth Trust, 1962,
vol. 1. p. 407.)

7. Latimer, *Remains*, pp. 297-309: 'A letter written to the king for
restoring again the liberty of reading the Holy Scriptures', 1 December
1530.

others. Several years were to elapse before Henry decided that it was wise to give his subjects the freedom to read the Bible and then, ironically, the version that was approved by the king was Tyndale's translation. As a sign of his esteem for Latimer, he was appointed a royal chaplain.

But Latimer soon wearied of court life. Before his appointment he had been in court a good deal and as a yeoman's son he found that court, with its luxury, endless intrigues and petty squabbles, was too tiring and it seemed fruitless ground for his preaching. Through the influence of friends at court he was presented with a country parish. Despite the protests and entreaties of those who liked his preaching he left London and, on 14 January 1531, he became Rector of West Kington, in Wiltshire. Surely the country people would be more receptive to the gospel than the aristocracy, he reasoned.

Ironically, Latimer's bishop was none other than Cardinal Campeggio, as West Kington lay in the diocese of Salisbury. But Campeggio had never set foot in his diocese — his only visit to England had been for Henry's divorce. In his absence the diocese was administered by the vicar-general, Richard Hiley. Latimer probably thought of West, Bishop of Ely, and remembered that West had banned him from preaching. Would he meet the same hostility in Wiltshire?

6. Parish priest

Wolsey's failure to obtain Henry's divorce had made the king more conscious than ever of the chain that bound him. Henry wished to free himself, not just from the domination of the pope, but also from the domination of the clergy in England. The question in his mind was: how could he do this? He was afraid that if he introduced changes of doctrine or practice, the teaching of Tyndale or Luther would reach the people.

As the king pondered over this, Thomas Cromwell, who had left the service of Wolsey and was rising in favour with Henry, made a suggestion. He pointed out that in the past kings had frequently revived long-forgotten laws and inflicted heavy penalties on people who had violated them. Now England had a law called *Praemunire* which had been passed in the fourteenth century and which sternly forbad all appeal to the court of Rome, all bulls from the pope, all excommunication, or anything that infringed the rights of the Crown. Any person breaking this law was to be put out of the king's protection, deprived of his property, arrested and brought for trial. This statute had lain like an old book on a shelf, unused and covered with dust. At Cromwell's suggestion, Henry took *Praemunire* up, dusted it and held it before clergy and people.

Wolsey, as he had performed his duties as papal legate, had trespassed upon the rights of the Crown. He had been condemned for this and had received justice. But what about the other clergy? They, too, had recognized this unlawful jurisdiction of Rome: they were as guilty as Wolsey.

Cromwell said to Henry, 'The statute of *Praemunire* condemns them as well as their leader.' Henry listened carefully, checked the facts with lawyers and found that Cromwell was right and all the clergy were guilty. He considered this an excellent way to free himself from the domination of the clergy and show them that he was indeed a king in his own right.

When the Convocation of Canterbury met in January 1531, Cromwell, as Secretary of State, entered the hall and took his seat among the bishops. Suddenly he rose and told the startled bishops that all their property and benefices were to be confiscated because they had submitted to the unconstitutional power of the dead cardinal.

'But the king himself told us to do these things and to obey Wolsey!' exclaimed the horrified bishops. 'Our resistance would have ruined us if we had dared to disobey.'

'That is of no consequence,' Cromwell replied, 'there was the law: you should obey the constitution of the country even at the peril of your lives.'

In terror, the bishops offered to pay a large sum of money to Henry but this was not what he wanted. The threat of confiscation was only to frighten them and make them pay an even higher ransom.

'My lords,' Cromwell said, 'in a petition that some of you presented to the pope not long ago, you called the king your *soul* and your *head*. Come then, expressly recognize the supremacy of the king over the church, and His Majesty, of his great goodness, will grant you a pardon.' This was what Henry had been aiming at from the beginning. If he became head of the church, who could dare to question his will in any ecclesiastical matter and would anyone have the insolence to refuse him the divorce that he had sought for so long?

The terrified clergy assembled and began to debate this new problem which they had to face. 'The words in the address to the pope,' said some, 'were a mere form, and had not the meaning ascribed to them.' 'The secular power has no voice in ecclesiastical matters,' declared the most zealous. 'To recognize the king as head of the church would be to overthrow the Catholic faith. . . . The head of the church is the pope.'

The debate lasted for days and as Henry's ministers pointed to the theocratic government of Israel a priest exclaimed, 'We oppose the New Testament to the Old; according to the gospel, Christ is Head of the church.' Strange words from people who had long spoken only of the pope as head of the church.

When they told the king this he said, 'Very well, I consent. If you declare me head of the church you may add *under God*.' The Bishops of Lincoln and Exeter went to see the king and beseech him to withdraw his demand but Henry refused even to see them. He had made up his mind, and the hierarchy must yield. The clergy implored the king's forgiveness and offered to pay him £144,000 — an enormous sum for those days. But Henry would not change his mind or draw back. It was not their money that he wanted but the power and authority that they possessed. In the draft of the document that assured them of the royal pardon, the king was described as 'the protector and supreme head of the church and clergy of England'.

The clergy were astounded by a statement which would annul their oath to the pope and abolish the supremacy of the Holy See of Rome. Day after day they debated the subject and various suggestions were made to try to change the wording so as to preserve the authority of the church. Henry refused to listen to any of their proposals or suggestions. Eventually, on 11 February 1531, Warham, Archbishop of Canterbury, declared that they would have to recognize the king as 'sole protector, only sovereign lord, and also, as far as by the law of Christ is lawful, supreme head of the English church'. Reluctantly the Convocation agreed to this wording and from the moment that this became a statute, the power of Rome was broken. Henry was now head of the church in England.

To purchase the king's pardon for their breach of *Praemunire*, the Convocation of Canterbury paid £100,000 into the royal coffers; later the Convocation of York paid nearly £19,000. By this clever move Henry not only made himself head of the church, but also began to drain away the vast store of money that the church had been accumulating for centuries. As the king had obtained what he wanted, he now pardoned the hierarchy for their breach of the law in recognizing Wolsey as papal legate. After the Commons had discussed the matter, this amnesty was extended to all the other clergy in England.

After putting the clergy firmly in their place, Henry then turned to Parliament. Sir Thomas More went to the Commons and showed them the decision of the universities concerning the king's marriage and the powers of the pope. Henry knew that he must tread very carefully with the people in England, since feelings ran high regarding the queen and he did not want a civil war on his hands. So the chancellor was instructed to tell the members to report to their counties and towns that the king did not desire this divorce for his own will or pleasure, but only because of his own conscience and for the succession of the Crown.

Shortly after this, several lords went to the queen and told her of the decision that condemned her marriage and urged her to accept the arbitration of a committee. Catherine replied firmly, 'I pray you, tell the king I say I am his lawful wife, and in that point I will abide until the court of Rome determine to the contrary.'

As the news spread throughout England there was great agitation among the people. Priests proclaimed that the end of the world was coming and that the Anti-Christ would soon appear. Everywhere, in towns and villages, castles and ale-houses, the one topic of conversation was the king's divorce and the new powers that he had suddenly assumed. The church, as they knew it, was shaking, and those who knew of the Continental Reformation were asking, 'Will England see the same changes as Germany?' Some feared this, while others longed that it might take place.

Henry now took another step. In July 1531, another deputation went to the queen at Windsor. She was informed that her marriage with Prince Arthur had been consummated and she could not therefore be the wife of her husband's brother. Catherine was told that she must leave Windsor and go either to a convent or to some country residence. Despite the shattering news Catherine remained calm. She said, 'Whereso-

ever I retire, nothing can deprive me of the title which
belongs to me. I shall always be His Majesty's wife.' She left
Windsor and eventually settled at Ampthill in Bedfordshire.
Henry never saw her again.

* * * * * * *

Hugh Latimer had been working hard for the last few years
and West Kington seemed just what he needed. He could have
some rest, he could preach freely, there was the parish work
to do but he would be free from the strain and vexation
which had surrounded him at Cambridge and the court. Most
of all, he would be free from the bitter controversy and long
debates which, while he enjoyed the latter, took a heavy toll
of energy and prevented him from preaching the Word. He
was well over forty now and felt less energetic than he had
done a few years previously.

As Latimer settled down, he saw things that reminded him
of his home at Thurcaston. Half a mile from the rectory
there was the famous Roman Fosse Way which leads through
Gloucester and Warwick, and past his father's farm on its way
to Lincoln. It must have seemed a real link with his childhood home.

Born in the country, Latimer had a heart for the needs of
the countryman, and he soon began to preach with zeal to
the people who worshipped at the little country church. But
the arrival of a man like Latimer, whose reputation as a
preacher had travelled all over England, could not take place
without causing a ferment in a quiet county like Wiltshire.
The neighbouring priests were alarmed lest this preacher of
heresy should corrupt the minds of their flocks. There were,
of course, those who had embraced the doctrines of the
Reformers and who still remembered the preaching of
William Tyndale ten years before when he lived in
Gloucestershire. They were elated at the prospect of hearing
and seeing this man who preached the truth from the Word
of God and wondered if he would be like Tyndale. The quiet
time that Latimer had looked forward to was not to last for

long.

* * * * * * *

Convocation, after it had swallowed the bitter pill of recognizing Henry as head of the church and had paid the enormous fine, then turned its spite to the ever-popular occupation of persecuting heretics and many suffered at its hands. Stokesley, the new Bishop of London, had his attention drawn to Latimer's preaching and, although Latimer was officially far from his grasp in another diocese, he proposed to try to have him brought before Convocation, together with Bilney and Crome, a London priest, to be tried for heretical preaching within his diocese. He was unsuccessful in reaching Latimer or Bilney, but the vindictive bishop was determined to wait until Latimer came near enough for him to grasp. Crome was at once brought for trial and, sad to say, like many other Reformers he recanted under the pressure of the bishops and reaffirmed his belief in the Roman dogma.

Latimer, meanwhile, had been drawn into a controversy with some of the neighbouring clergy. Because he preached the gospel they hated him. Four miles from West Kington there was a village called Marshfield and here Latimer had preached and condemned the conduct of prelates. Without question he was incensed at the cruelty of Stokesley to the people brought before him. Reports of Latimer's sermon reached the clergy in exaggerated and distorted form. He had preached on the text: 'All that ever came before Me were thieves and robbers.' According to the reports, he had strongly asserted that all bishops, popes, rectors and vicars were thieves and robbers and that all the hemp in England was insufficient for hanging them. He had declared that Peter had no supremacy over the other apostles, that all Christians were priests and that baptism was of no avail unless men lived lives worthy of their Christian profession. As frequently happens, people had taken a few of his words here and there and brought a garbled message to the clergy, or else malicious men had deliberately distorted his preaching.

To be fair, Latimer had not yet learned enough Reformed theology to make such assertions. In any case, statements such as these were not typical of him or of the English Reformers in general, but of the extremists. He was a slow but steady learner and as he studied Scripture he saw more clearly the things that needed correction in the church. He saw, too, the different changes in doctrine that were needed, but this was a gradual and slow process for one brought up in the cradle of Rome. Latimer had certainly not reached the point where he was prepared to make statements like those which were attributed to him.

However, the sermon was a bold one and it provided excellent material for the priests to bring various charges against him. One of the priests, William Sherwood, from the parish of Derham near West Kington, wrote Latimer a long letter, in which he described his sermon at Marshfield as his 'insane satire'. The letter was a mixture of pretended courtesy and offensive rudeness, but it also contained much bitterness. Latimer replied in a blunt and indignant style and he had much justification for this. It would appear that Sherwood had regarded himself as the great oracle of the county until Latimer's arrival, and that his action had been partly prompted by jealousy since the man he regarded as a rival had now taken the stage. While Sherwood disliked the letter he received, he was a little more cautious when he replied to it. It would seem that Sherwood had overrated his strength when he took on Latimer. He failed to realize that the best wits of Cambridge had set themselves against him to no avail. A discreet retirement from the fight was Sherwood's best policy and he reluctantly withdrew.

About midsummer Latimer visited London. He had been asked to do this by his friends; it is possible that Cromwell, even, and Dr Butts, the king's doctor, wanted him to preach there. Many others longed to hear him preach again. His words brought them hope and spiritual life. He preached first in Kent at the request of the parish priest, but knew that Stokesley was so adamant against any Reformed doctrine that he declined to preach in London. Finally a group of merchants came and entreated him to preach at St Mary Abchurch. They said, 'We have great hunger and thirst of the Word of God, and of ghostly [spiritual] doctrine.' Latimer had no intention of defying Stokesley's authority, but neither did he wish to avoid the responsibility that lay on his shoulders as a preacher of the gospel. He had declined to preach a number of times but now felt that he must agree, whatever the bishop's opinion. He told the merchants that he had no licence from the Bishop of London to preach, the only licence that he possessed being from the University of Cambridge. Only when he was satisfied that all precautions had been taken, that no deception was practised and the incumbent of the church was fully aware of what was to take place, did he agree to preach.

He was received with great courtesy by the parson and the curate. Latimer had the feeling that 'it was a train and trap laid before him, to the intent that Stokesley, or some other pertaining to him, should have been there to take him in his sermon'.[1] But this suspicion made him all the more anxious to preach with boldness. The text on which he preached was: 'Ye are not under the law.' 'What,' Latimer said, 'Christians not under the law! Not subject to the law! Surely this is a dangerous saying, if it be not rightly understood, sounding as if Christians were at liberty to break the laws. What if the adversaries of St Paul had so understood them, and had accused St Paul before the Bishop of London for preaching them? If my lord of London would have listened to St Paul declaring his own opinion of his own words, then he should have escaped and his opponents should have been rebuked; but if he had given sentence according to the representatives of his accusers, then good St Paul must have borne a faggot on his back. . . . Oh, it had been a goodly sight to have seen St Paul thus!'

Judges, Latimer maintained, should be very careful in acting against any preachers and should place little value on the reports of ignorant and biased listeners who either mis-

1. *Remains*, p. 327.

understood or deliberately misinterpreted what they had heard. Latimer obviously had Sherwood much in mind as he spoke. He went on to talk of the abuses and superstitions that were widespread at this time. He is even said to have spoken with disrespect of the 'sacrament of the altar', but this is unlikely as Latimer's doctrinal views had not altered enough to cause him to have any doubts about this.

A sermon like this could not fail to excite Stokesley's indignation. He regarded it as a direct attack upon himself and there was much justification for this view as he, in collaboration with Sir Thomas More, had commenced a violent campaign of illegal persecution. Stokesley tried to get Henry's anger roused against Latimer by declaring that his sermon was a defence of the heretics then on trial. But Henry refused to rise to the bait and Latimer returned safely to West Kington.

Although Latimer was safe in his country parish, his mind was far away as he wondered anxiously how his old friend Bilney was faring. In the spring of 1531 'little Bilney' had called together his friends at Cambridge and said farewell for the last time. 'I must needs go up to Jerusalem,' he told them. With tears they said farewell and commended him to God's care and keeping. They realized that persuasion was useless.

Bilney, who had continued to suffer agonies of remorse, had finally resolved that it was his duty, whatever the risk might be, to preach openly those doctrines which he had twice denied. He went first to Norfolk, his native county, and visited groups of Christians and preached in the fields. He confessed and lamented his former cowardice and warned them not to be misled by their friends nor to yield if they were brought for trial. He then moved south and it is believed that he visited London, since he was seen at Greenwich. Wherever Bilney went, he distributed copies of Tyndale's New Testament.

Finally, the Bishop of Norwich caught him after he had moved north again. Bilney was a relapsed heretic taken in the act of distributing heretical books, so there was no question about his fate. A writ for burning him at the stake was speedily obtained from Sir Thomas More. More is reported to have said, 'Burn him first and then ask me for a bill of indemnity' — a clear breach of the law and of justice. After a trial that was a mere farce, Bilney was sentenced, degraded from the priesthood and handed over to the sheriff for burning.

A few of his friends from Cambridge came over to see and comfort him the night before his death. Among them was Matthew Parker, later Archbishop of Canterbury. 'Tomorrow,' said one friend, 'the fire will make you feel its devouring fierceness, but the comfort of God's Holy Spirit will cool it for your everlasting refreshing.' As Bilney listened he put his finger into the flame of the lamp. 'What are you doing?' his friends asked. 'Nothing,' Bilney replied. 'I am only trying my flesh; tomorrow God's rods shall burn my whole body in the fire. . . . I am persuaded, by God's holy Word and the experience of the martyrs, that when the flames consume me, I shall not feel them. Howsoever this stubble of my body shall be wasted by it, a pain for the time is followed by joy unspeakable.' Bilney then quoted, 'When thou walkest through the fire, thou shalt not be burnt' (Isaiah 43:2). [2] His friends never forgot those words.

The next day, 19 August, he was led to a deep hollow outside the gate of the city of Norwich called the *Lollards' Pit*. This, with the rising ground, made a natural amphitheatre which was covered with onlookers. Bilney fell down and prayed and then embraced the stake. He was chained to it and the flames were kindled. 'Good folk,' Bilney said to the onlookers, 'be not angry against these men for my sake; as though they be the authors of my death, it is not they.'

Poor Bilney was miserably scorched as the wind blew the fire away from him before the flames were strong enough to destroy him. Even in the agony of death he was heard to utter the name of Jesus and to say 'Credo' (I believe) several

2. Bilney's Bible, which is kept in the library of Corpus Christi College, Cambridge has these verses (Isaiah 43. 1-3) marked with a pen in the margin.

times, and so he glorified his Saviour even in the flames. At
length the fire put Bilney out of his agony.

History has not given Bilney his rightful place in the work
that he did at Cambridge and in England for the Reformation.
While he was gentle, timid and unassuming, his friends knew
his real worth. If, like Peter, he denied his Lord several times,
at his final trial and death he was unflinching and constant.

When the news reached Latimer he was inconsolable. He
recalled the day when 'little Bilney' came to him and he had
first learnt the way of salvation from his lips. He remembered
those walks around Cambridge when he had plied Bilney with
questions and he had answered patiently and confidently.
Latimer's mind flashed back to those meetings at the White
Horse tavern when Bilney, as he expounded God's Word, had
seemed like one inspired. Now he was dead. Apart from his
grief, Bilney's death forced Latimer to face the fact that it
might not be long before he, too, had to lay down his life
for Christ. It gave him an increased sense of urgency in his
preaching.

There was need for this, since the death of Bilney was like
the first taste of blood to wolves. Stokesley and More were
both eager for more. One martyrdom would not satisfy these
men and they, together with Gardiner and Lee, commenced a
widespread persecution. It would appear that the prelates felt
guilty towards Rome for acknowledging the king as head of
the church and believed they could only expiate their faults
by sacrificing Reformers.

To adapt the expression falsely ascribed to Latimer and
apply it to Sir Thomas More, all the trees in England would
be insufficient to burn all the heretics that he was able to
capture. The man who had once penned the noble lines of
Utopia had developed into a fanatic of the first order and his
treatment of all suspected of heresy can only be described as
bestial. To More in his later days, every other man whom he
encountered was a possible heretic. He behaved like a man
possessed. Despite the fact that More was chancellor and a
skilled lawyer, this man who had every law in England at his
fingertips now proceeded to break the law. It was not until

he resigned as chancellor that heresy was made high treason, but More acted as if the law was on his side and treated people accused of heresy as criminals. At his home in Chelsea there was a tree in the garden known as the 'Jesus Tree' or 'Tree of Truth' where heretics were tied and whipped with More's own hands. A leather merchant, John Tewkesbury, was whipped in the autumn of 1531 in More's garden. As he refused to recant, More had cords tied round his head and tightened until the blood started from his eyes. Tewkesbury was then taken to the Tower and stretched on the rack until at last he recanted. He was then dismissed but was later found preaching and was tried and burnt at Smithfield in December. All this was done without any writ from the king authorizing More's or Stokesley's actions. While Henry must take his share of the blame for the cruelty in his reign, Rome was the first and greatest offender.

Stokesley was not a man who would let an enemy slip through his fingers. While Latimer appeared to be safe at West Kington, the wheels of the hierarchy were turning and Stokesley was setting in motion that machinery which he hoped would bring Latimer within his clutches. Several of Latimer's friends knew of the bishop's evil intentions and advised him to leave England and seek refuge on the Continent. For a while Latimer felt so despondent that he nearly took their advice. He wrote several letters to Baynton, lord of the manor at Bromeham, near to West Kington, with whom Latimer had become friendly, and sought his advice. Baynton was, of course, a courtier and he recommended caution and submission. As he pointed out, it was not for an unlearned man and a layman to give his opinion in these matters. He also stated that he knew little of the doctrinal matters to which Latimer referred. One writer has said that it is this plea 'of ignorance, assuming the garb of modesty and prudence, which has always been the grand obstacle to every reformation'. If there were more people wholeheartedly behind the leaders of reform, reformation would take place more speedily and more frequently.

It is true that Latimer still had much to learn and he was

anxious to retain the ceremonies of the church, but he wanted to purify them from the mass of superstition that was woven round them. However, day by day, the gulf that separated Latimer and the defenders of the church was getting wider and wider. Although he failed to realize it, he was becoming increasingly Bible-centred, a man who would lift his Bible and ask, 'What do the Scriptures say about this?'

While he pondered over these matters, Latimer was startled one day by a messenger who brought him an order to appear before Bishop Stokesley to answer for the crimes he had committed by preaching in his diocese. 'I should have fled to the Continent!' Latimer exclaimed. 'What will become of me now?'

7. Persecution and weakness

1532 – 1533

The horse stepped into a hole in the road and stumbled, and Latimer clutched at the rein to avoid falling from the saddle. He could not blame the horse; it was as tired as he was and both were frozen by the icy January wind. Still, he had reached the outskirts of London and his journey was almost over. The question in his mind was: what lay ahead?

It had been a long journey and Latimer had felt the strain, the more so since he had been brooding over all that had taken place during the past year. He was also uneasy as he wondered what the bishop would do with him when he arrived.

He had wasted no time after he received the order to appear before Stokesley, but his thoughts returned to the country rectory that he had left behind. He had been there a year now and when he began his work he had hoped that he would have rest and peace, but instead he had found that debate and controversy had followed him.as he faithfully preached the Word. 'Now what awaits me?' was the question uppermost in his mind. He remembered Bilney and wondered whether he would return to his country rectory in safety or whether he would suffer the same fate as 'little Bilney'.

Latimer was still orthodox regarding the central doctrines of the Roman church. His convictions were unchanged on the mass. He had preached against superstition and abuses but these were not doctrinal heresies. Nevertheless the clergy knew that he was a leader of those who supported Reformed doctrines.

When Latimer reached London he was immediately placed on trial before Stokesley and several other bishops. They questioned him and tried to trip him up in various ways, but he described his experience when Bilney had visited him, and then used all the skill which he had employed at Cambridge to give answers that frustrated them.

After Latimer had been examined for several days, he noticed that most of the furniture in the room in which he was being questioned had been moved round. Previously there had been a fire burning in the grate. Now there was no fire, but a cloth had been draped across the fireplace. Latimer listened carefully and heard the squeak of a pen on paper. It puzzled him until one of the bishops said, 'I pray you, Master Latimer, speak out; I am very thick of hearing and here be many that sit far off.' He then realized the motive behind this request. Someone hidden in the chimney was taking down every word that he uttered. All the skill and all the wit with which God had endowed him were needed that day to prevent him from falling into the bishops' trap.

The trial dragged on for six weeks and was then referred to Convocation. On 11 March 1532, Latimer was brought before Convocation either to admit his heresy or subscribe to the abuses which he himself had condemned. Three times he refused to subscribe. Archbishop Warham then excommunicated Latimer and he was detained at Lambeth while they decided what should be done with him. He was, after all, one of the king's chaplains and Henry had already shown how ruthless he could be if the hierarchy upset him.

The articles Latimer was asked to sign are too numerous to be looked at in detail, but one or two will suffice to show the type of doctrine and practice that he was expected to support. First, he denied purgatory, then he denied that souls in purgatory are helped by the mass, prayers or alms. He also denied that the saints in heaven pray for us as mediators and that these saints should be worshipped. Latimer refuted most firmly the idea that the 'power of the keys' given to Peter remained with the Bishop of Rome, even when he lived wickedly. He denied, too, that in every one of the seven sacraments grace is obtained by those who rightly receive them.

These examples give some idea of the questions that Latimer had been asked and obviously they had been drawn up with great cunning. If the questions had been taken separately, he would probably not have denied any of them, but grouped together he realized that they supported and sanctioned all the abuses and superstitions against which he was fighting. Moreover, they had no scriptural support.

Ten days later Latimer again appeared before Convocation. While he had been waiting he had suffered great mental anguish and was well aware that his life was in danger. In his perplexity he wrote to Warham and admitted that images and pilgrimages are lawful. It was also lawful to pray to saints and to care for souls in purgatory but, he emphasized, these things were voluntary, that is they were not commanded by God's Word and should be kept in moderation. The priorities must remain in their rightful place. Latimer protested, 'I dare not subscribe the bare propositions submitted to me, because I am unwilling, by any little authority of mine, to perpetuate this popular superstition, lest in so doing I should bring damnation on myself. . . there are occasions on which one must obey God rather than man.'[1]

Latimer's arguments were unanswerable, but behind the scenes others were pulling strings. Butts and Cromwell were trying to get the prelates to moderate their demands and also hoped to persuade Latimer to compromise and meet them halfway.

He was again brought before his judges on 21 March, and the bishops then offered to release him from the sentence of excommunication, if he would subscribe to the eleventh and fourteenth articles and then apologize for what had taken place. Latimer agreed to this and hoped that he would be speedily restored to freedom and to his country parish. The bishops, however, had no intention of letting him off as easily as that. He had to go on his knees and apologize to Stokesley and read a humiliating confession to Convocation, after which he had humbly to ask to be absolved from excommunication.

Convocation was in no hurry to release a man like Latimer

1. Foxe, *Acts and Monuments*, vol. vii. p.457.

and it remanded him for three weeks. Doubtless it hoped to obtain further confessions from him. He had to come before them again on 10 April and according to the existing records of Convocation[2] he then signed all the articles apart from the eleventh and fourteenth — but this is doubtful.

It is believed that Cromwell advised Latimer to appeal from Convocation to the king. Henry is also believed to have counselled him to submit himself to the bishops; their doctrine must be his doctrine and their practice his practice. It is highly probable that he did accept the king's advice and sign the humiliating articles. As one writer has said, it was 'the darkest page in Latimer's history'. Soon after this he was absolved by Stokesley and released.

We may well ask, why did Latimer change like this? From adamant refusal, he appears to have suddenly weakened. The strong-minded yeoman's son, who was prepared to face a king and stand for the truth, seems to have crumbled and become weaker than Bilney. But physically he was less robust and in his letter to Warham he tells how his health had de-teriorated: 'My head is so out of frame, and my whole body so weak.' In his letters during that winter and spring he con-tinually complained of pains in the head. Apart from the constant interrogation, his state of health goes a long way to explain — while it does not excuse — his sudden change and submission.

Latimer must have felt deeply depressed when he was finally released. Bilney had stood firm; why had he acted like Peter and denied his Lord? Yet before his return to West Kington he had another surprise, one that made a great im-pression on him, especially in view of the fate that he had so narrowly escaped.

Three friends asked him if he would come with them to visit a condemned heretic, James Bainham. This man had been sentenced and was to be burnt at the stake the next

2. The original records for this are incomplete and mutilated. The records that exist are a reconstruction brought from a variety of sources so we cannot place much confidence in them.

day. Bainham was a lawyer and well known for his charity
and piety; he was also a devout reader of Scripture. He had
read Tyndale's books and listened to Latimer preach in
London. Bainham had suffered at the hands of More; he had
also been racked at the Tower but had remained constant. It
is recorded that when he was examined by More and
Stokesley, Bainham's answers on the doctrines of purgatory
and the invocation of saints had shown a knowledge of the
Bible that would have made many of the Reformers blush.
Finally, Bainham had recanted and been released, but his
conscience had given him no rest and he had gone to the local
church and stood up with Tyndale's New Testament in one
hand and had confessed that he had denied his Saviour. He
had warned the people to beware of yielding in weakness as
he had done. He had been promptly rearrested and condemned to death.

When Latimer visited him in Newgate prison he found
Bainham sitting 'with a book and a wax candle in his hand,
praying and reading thereupon'.[3] After his recent release
from prison Latimer was cautious but also curious, and asked
Bainham why he was in gaol and about to die. When he
found that Bainham had spoken out against Thomas-à-Becket,
the great saint of the South of England, and had called him a
traitor, Latimer was shocked. 'I spoke also against purgatory,'
Bainham said, 'that there was no such thing; but that it
picked men's purses.' This horrified Latimer, since it
appeared to him that Bainham had decided in his heart that
he must die, and he warned him to 'beware of vain-glory'
and throwing away his life needlessly.

Before he left, Latimer advised him to take his death
quietly and patiently and Bainham thanked him heartily.
Then Bainham, as if with intuition, said, 'I likewise do exhort
you to stand to the defence of the truth; for you that shall be
left behind had need of comfort.' Next day Bainham was
burnt and he remained constant to the end.

His words had not been wasted on Latimer, who realized

3. Strype, *Eccl. Mem.* from Harleian MSS, p. 422.

that Bainham had put a finger on his weak spot. He must stand constant in defence of the truth and he must know more clearly what Scripture taught about the doctrines that Bainham had denied. In the coming months Bainham's words echoed through his mind and we can imagine him declaring, 'Never again! If I am to die, I will die like Bilney or Bainham rather than deny the truth.'

* * * * * * *

Soon after Latimer returned to West Kington the legal powers of Convocation were annulled. Nothing could now be passed without the king's approval. The day after this became law, 16 May 1532, Sir Thomas More resigned as chancellor. Now that the church had fallen and become subject to the king, he could not bear to sit as chancellor and see her without her former glory.

Henry's long-drawn-out divorce proceedings were nearing their end. He had waited with great patience for some news from the papal court. But a king who elevated himself to be 'head of the English church' was regarded with strong disfavour at Rome. Henry decided that he would go ahead and marry Anne Boleyn, after he had obtained Convocation's approval. Unfortunately Warham died in August 1532 and Henry was shrewd enough to realize that a new archbishop would never be appointed if he provoked the pope by marrying. He must first find a successor to Warham and have him officially consecrated as archbishop with the papal bulls and he would then be recognized by clergy and people alike. The big question in Henry's mind was: whom should he choose as archbishop? He must be a 'king's man', that is, one who would obey Henry's wishes rather than the pope's and one who would be favourable to the marriage.

His choice fell on Thomas Cranmer. Cranmer, as we have seen, had a clear knowledge of the way of salvation and had steeped himself in Scripture. England, for the first time in centuries, would have a truly Christian archbishop and one who was wholeheartedly in favour of the Reformation. In

God's sovereignty, Cranmer was placed in a position where he could make decisions, direct the findings and actions of many others in the church, place Reformers in key positions, reform the doctrine and practices of the Anglican church and — last but not least — where he would have the ear of the king. By prudence and tact he could try to move Henry to help the Reformation, apart from influencing him in his spiritual life.

It was an enormous responsibility, yet there was no one in England better qualified for the office than Cranmer. His learning, piety, honesty and knowledge of the Bible all qualified him for the work. Cranmer's first reaction was horror at such responsibility. He was a scholar and his natural home was the study and the lecture hall. At first he declined the office, but accepted it after Henry repeated his request.

When Henry initially asked Cranmer to become archbishop, he had been on the Continent on a mission for the king. He deliberately delayed his return in the hope that, since Henry was an impatient man, he would choose some other clergyman rather than wait for his return. When at Cambridge, Cranmer had married and had been forced to resign his fellowship. After a short while his wife died and he was then reinstated as a fellow. While in Germany he stayed with one of the German Reformers, Osiander, and there he met and fell in love with Margaret, the niece of Osiander's wife. Before returning to England Cranmer married Margaret but, knowing Henry's views on married clergy, he left her on the Continent until he saw what things were like in England. Later he brought her to England but she was never presented at court.

Consecrating Cranmer as archbishop presented Henry with a fresh problem. 'If I accept this office,' Cranmer said, 'I must receive it from the hands of the pope, and this my conscience will not permit me to do. . . neither the pope nor any other foreign prince has authority in this realm.' Henry had not thought of this. He asked Cranmer if it could be proved from Scripture and Cranmer replied, 'Holy Scripture and the fathers support the supreme authority of kings in their kingdoms, and thus prove the claims of the pope to be a miserable usurpation.'

Although these were mainly Cranmer's personal conscientious objections, they sent Henry further down the road of reform. Before this he had not considered consecrating bishops without papal approval. After conferring with the lawyers, he decided this was possible if the pope sent the necessary bulls for the inauguration of the new archbishop. The pontiff, who was only too pleased to have some part in the ecclesiastical matters of England, sent them promptly to Cranmer.

On the day that Cranmer was consecrated as archbishop, he took an unprecedented step by breaking with medieval practice. On 30 March 1533, he called the leading clergy to Westminster and read them a paper in which he protested that he would not bind himself by oath to anything contrary to the law of God. He refused to be bound in anything concerning liberty of speech and the reformation of all things that needed reforming in the Church of England. Cranmer insisted that his protest be repeated at each stage of the ceremony and so he nailed his colours to the mast.

Cranmer's protest was an act of Christian decision. His time in Germany had been most profitable and he had learned much from the German Reformers. Now he sought to apply it in the new office that he had accepted, since he was determined to be as biblical as possible. The hearts of men like Latimer must have beat faster with new hope. At last England had a leader who was resolved to bring the church into line with New Testament principles.

But one flaw appeared in all this: Cranmer finished by reading the customary oath to St Peter and the holy apostolic church of Rome. Henry no doubt insisted on this. Yet for one who began so well and who wished to break with Romish practices, would it not have been possible to persuade Henry to allow him to drop this oath? This flaw in Cranmer's character, pious and well grounded in the Scriptures as he was, revealed itself repeatedly when he was under pressure.

* * * * * * *

Henry had asked the pope for the necessary bulls to consecrate Cranmer in January 1533, but soon after his
messenger had left for Rome a bull arrived from the pope
ordering Henry to dismiss Anne from the court. The emperor,
who was Catherine's nephew, had persuaded the pope that
this should be done. It was fortunate that Henry had already
sent his messenger for the bulls to consecrate Cranmer. The
tone of these letters was more than Henry could bear. To him
it was the crowning insult of the whole long-drawn-out affair.
For this reason, and another more pressing one, he decided
not to wait any longer. Anne was pregnant and this would
soon become obvious. She had overcome her earlier scruples
of conscience as she saw the divorce approaching. In January
1533 Henry was married to Anne privately by one of his
chaplains, Rowland Lee. The marriage was kept secret for a
time, lest news of it should reach Rome. If the pope knew, he
would refuse to send the bulls to consecrate Cranmer.

The bulls arrived, Cranmer was consecrated and the final
steps were taken for the divorce. Parliament passed a statute
which stated, 'The Crown of England was imperial, and the
nation a complete body in itself, with full power to give
justice in all causes, spiritual and temporal.' Appeals to Rome
were forbidden and anyone attempting to obtain a bull or
appeal to Rome was subject to heavy penalties.

Soon after his consecration, Cranmer was instructed to
hold a court at Dunstable and this finally settled the question
that had dragged on for six years. Sentence of divorce was
pronounced and the marriage between Henry and Catherine
declared null and void. A few days later Cranmer confirmed
Henry's marriage to Anne and on 28 May she was conducted
to the Tower in state. On 1 June she was crowned at Westminster Abbey and presented to the nation in all splendour.
By then it was difficult to hide the fact that she was
pregnant.

Did Anne have any qualms as she took her seat on the
throne? As she sat there in pomp and grandeur, did she

consider the princess whose place she had taken? Might not the same fate befall her one day? In her new role as queen, Anne still felt attracted to the gospel, just as she had been when with Margaret of Valois. Soon after she ascended the throne, she used her influence to help some who, she knew, were devoted to spreading the gospel message. Foxe records that John Lambert, still in prison, was pardoned as a result of the coming of Queen Anne.

The pope's fury knew no bounds when he learned that Henry and Anne were married. He annulled the marriage and declared it to be unlawful. He also threatened to excommunicate them both unless they separated by the end of September. But the irrevocable step had been taken; it was too late for this. Henry refused to turn back. On 7 September Anne gave birth to a daughter, Elizabeth. While Henry had hoped fervently that the child would be a boy, he still felt that heaven approved of the marriage that Rome had refused and he received the baby with joy. Anne was young and could soon have more children. The next child would surely be the prince for whom he longed.

8. *Royal favour*

'Yes, I maintain that Our Lady was a sinner like all other mortals and that she ought not to be worshipped, nor should we worship any of the saints!'[1] Latimer's voice rang through the crowded church.

He had been comparatively silent since his return from London the previous year. His close escape had shaken him. Now, in March 1533, he was in Bristol preaching in the churches of St Nicholas and the Black Friars. As he looked round he could see many shocked faces in the congregation, but beside these there were others that looked thoughtful. He could tell that some of his listeners were pondering over what he had said.

The people of Bristol had more than their share of religion in the sixteenth century. The city, which ranked with the four other large cities of England – London, York, Coventry and Norwich – had about six thousand inhabitants. Like all large cities of this era, it was filled with religious houses, abbeys, convents, monasteries and chantries. It observed a large number of religious festivals and people had become accustomed to false Christianity, but Latimer's words had the ring of truth about them.

Soon the city hummed with the news: this outspoken preacher was attacking the church and, worse still, the Virgin Mary. For a thousand years the cult of Mary worship had been growing. By the sixteenth century she was not just a saint; she had been elevated to such a position that it would be no exaggeration to say that, for the ordinary man or woman, she had been deified. Now this country priest

1. Strype, *Eccl. Mem.* vol. i, p. 248.

denounced the worship of Mary! Surely this was heresy and an unforgivable sin!

Bristol quickly became divided; some defended Latimer while others attacked him fiercely. The hostile party among the priests sent a letter to the Archdeacon of Worcester and demanded that Latimer be forbidden to preach in Bristol. But he had not gone there seeking an opportunity to preach, he had been invited by several priests and he had a further invitation from the Mayor of Bristol to preach at Easter. Bristol was a wealthy city, so wealthy that Henry IV had levied a tax on all who were worth twenty pounds a year, because of the luxurious fashion in which their wives were dressed. A city composed of rich merchants does not take kindly to interference from a distant hierarchy; it is much too independent.

The people were furious with the priests for interfering. It was almost Easter and their intervention meant that Latimer could not come with his new teaching. He had been forbidden to preach in Bristol without the bishop's licence.

Latimer was indignant at being prevented from preaching or defending his own teaching after he had been denounced as a heretic. His words had been taken and distorted. The controversy raged for months and theological discussions were heard everywhere: some supported Latimer while others still denounced him as a heretic. Not only had he attacked the worship of Mary, but he had condemned pilgrimages and other superstitious practices. Latimer did not remain quietly at his country church. Instead he brought his enemies before the Mayor and council of Bristol and challenged them to prove the truth of their accusations. This they were unable to do. 'They had both place and time,' he said, 'to slander me and to belie me, but they had neither place nor time to hear me, when I was ready to justify all that I had said.'[2]

Some good came out of this as one of Latimer's opponents, John Hilsey, Prior of the Black Friars, came to discuss the new teaching and was eventually convinced of the truth of

2. *Chapter House Papers*: unfinished letter of Latimer.

Latimer's words. Hilsey then became his friend and faithful supporter.

The Bristol controversy raged so fiercely that its echoes reverberated as far as London and reached Cromwell's ears. He appointed commissioners to investigate the whole affair and report to the Privy Council. Latimer's enemies had overstepped the mark; by denouncing him as a heretic they had laid themselves open to prosecution. In the debates they had condemned Parliament's proceedings and even censured Henry's divorce and his marriage to Anne. Many had spoken in a way that was not far short of treason. One priest in particular, a man named William Hubbardin — who has been described as 'the great clerical buffoon of the day' — had even maintained the supremacy and infallibility of the papal see and made various comments about the king and Parliament which angered many loyal subjects in Bristol. Hubbardin, 'the Don Quixote of Roman Catholicism', wandered over England extolling the pope at the expense of the king, and denouncing men like Luther, Tyndale and Latimer. During a visit to West Kington he preached against Latimer, but while in the pulpit he danced, hopped and leaped about as if it were a stage and disgusted many of his hearers.

The commissioners worked thoroughly and sent all the evidence to Cromwell. The Mayor of Bristol imprisoned many of the priests and others conveniently disappeared from the neighbourhood. Hubbardin's vulgar speeches caused him to be jailed. As one old writer has said, 'The champions of the church began to discover, to their sad discomfiture, that the good old days, when a heretic might be pleasantly hunted to death, were gone.' The clergy also found that they could no longer act in such a high-handed manner. The new laws had changed the position of the Church of England.

In every way Latimer's enemies were beaten. They had succeeded in banning him from preaching without the bishop's licence but Cranmer, who was archbishop, gave him a licence to preach anywhere in his province, which included Bristol. Latimer later returned there to preach and in the autumn Cranmer also visited the city, where he remained for some time and preached in St Augustine's Abbey and other churches. It must have been a comfort to Latimer to know that he had a friend in Cranmer. He had been concerned at the king's possible reaction to all that had happened. Was Henry now prejudiced against him because of false reports? Thanks to Cranmer there was no cause for such concern, for he convinced Henry that Latimer had not broken the law or said anything indiscreet, and he therefore still retained the royal favour.

Latimer's discussion with Bainham was bearing fruit. The six months' controversy showed him that he could no longer hold fast to the old traditions. It became clear that his position was untenable. As he left the medieval teachings behind he realized that he could not compromise. It was reform or nothing and the only way for reform was back to the Scriptures. For too long he had cherished the idea that all that was needed to purge the church was the removal of the gross abuses that had sprung up over the centuries. He saw more clearly that every teaching and ritual must have a biblical basis. Even some of his adversaries' statements made him take a closer look at what he believed. Hubbardin had condemned the 'new learning as being of the devil, and not of God'. Latimer knew from experience that this was untrue, and now saw that the Bible was the touchstone for all teaching. The condemnation of his enemies drove him to search the Scriptures more often and with greater earnestness so that he might understand more clearly what they taught.

Cranmer's new powers were soon felt by Latimer's enemy Stokesley, Bishop of London. In October 1533 Latimer again went to London but was not on trial this time. He preached in the church of the Augustinian Friars, even though Stokesley had forbidden all preachers to officiate anywhere in his diocese without his special licence. Latimer not only lacked the licence but had also been mentioned in the episcopal document. He did, however, have Cranmer's licence to preach anywhere in his province. George Brown, Prior of the Augustinian monastery (who later became the first Protestant Archbishop of Dublin), gave him the pulpit in his priory.

Stokesley was furious when he heard of this and issued another order forbidding anyone to preach without his licence and threatening to punish any clergy who allowed Hugh Latimer to enter their church or religious house.

But Latimer did not fear Stokesley, as he had risen high in the king's favour and been appointed, together with Cromwell and Cranmer, to deal with the case of Elizabeth Barton, the 'Maid of Kent'. When a direct frontal attack fails in war, experienced leaders know that the best way of beating the enemy is to go round and attack from the rear, where he least expects it. The Roman hierarchy was quick to adopt these tactics to try to beat the king and the Reformers.

In the village of Aldington in Kent this young woman, Elizabeth Barton, was prone to what would appear to have been severe attacks of epilepsy. She uttered incoherent and unintelligible sentences and then fell to the ground stiff and lifeless. The local people believed that she was filled with the Holy Spirit, and the rector of the parish resolved to take advantage of this to gain money and reputation. He told her that if she failed to make known this gift from heaven, she would be guilty of sinning against the Holy Spirit. A neighbouring monk was also cunning enough to see how the girl could be used to assist the Roman party. He informed Elizabeth that the church was exposed to great danger from the Reformers but that God, who defends His church by the humblest people, had raised her up to protect what the king, the Reformers and Parliament all sought to destroy.

The girl was much flattered and, overcome by pride, began to regard her attacks as divine visitations. Many pilgrims came to the village and Elizabeth proved herself an apt pupil of the priests. She claimed to have visions and revelations of heaven, hell and purgatory. In the controversies that raged concerning the royal divorce, papal supremacy and the growth of the English heretics, the monks of Canterbury called upon her to defend the faith as the advocate of heaven. Elizabeth declared judgement on Henry for his divorce and on all who in any way interfered with the church.

The priests were careful to ensure that the stage was

properly set for Elizabeth Barton. In the fields of her local parish stood an old chapel which contained an image of the Virgin. The rector suggested she should tell the people that the Virgin would cure her of her illness. She was carried to the chapel with pomp and placed before the image. A crisis came upon her, her tongue hung from her mouth, her eyes started from their sockets and a voice was heard speaking of the terrors of hell. Suddenly there came a transformation and in a sweet voice she described the joys of paradise. [3] The ecstasy ended and Elizabeth came to herself declaring that she was completely cured and that God had told her to become a nun.

As soon as the fulfilment of Elizabeth's prophecy regarding her healing became known, her fame spread far and wide. She entered a convent and became the popular mouthpiece of the Roman party. She was also the centre of the opposition to the policy of Cranmer as well as the preaching of Latimer and the other Reformers. The nun had been in contact with both Wolsey and Warham before their deaths. Fisher and Sir Thomas More regarded her with awe and gave much respect to her revelations. It is believed that she was even in contact with the pope. Throughout England the friars were her champions; they quoted her and pointed to her as God's mouthpiece. Just as Joan of Arc, the Maid of Orleans, had been considered to be God's oracle to raise the French people against the English, so this nun was used by the Roman party to alert people to the dangers that threatened the church from the king and the Reformers. Elizabeth Barton continued her prophecies for some time and, strangely enough, the fiery-tempered Henry was, for once, very tolerant despite her predictions that he would fall if he married Anne. Months passed and all was well: the rise of Mary to the throne, as predicted by the nun, had not taken place.

But Cromwell and Cranmer realized that the danger to the country grew rapidly. It was no longer just superstition for

3. Cranmer, *Letters and Remains* (Parker Society), p. 273.

the masses, but a definite plot to overthrow Henry. Not only were Catherine and Mary in communication with Elizabeth, but so were Margaret Plantagenet, Countess of Salisbury, and her children, who represented the White Rose. The Wars of the Roses had torn England apart in the previous century, before the Tudors gained the throne. The country dare not risk another civil war.

Elizabeth Barton was arrested together with the leaders of the priests and brought before Cromwell, Cranmer and Latimer. For some time the priests remained silent but Elizabeth realized the enormity of her offence and confessed everything. 'I never had a vision in all my life,' she admitted, 'whatever I said was of my own imagination; I invented it to please the people about me and to attract the homage of the world.' It was impossible for the priests to deny their guilt and they too confessed all. They were imprisoned and, the following year, sentenced to death for treason. In April 1534, Elizabeth Barton was taken to Tyburn gallows in the midst of a crowd of people. On the scaffold she admitted that she was the cause not only of her own death, but of all those with her. Such was the superstition among the Catholics that her name was still in great favour among them in the reign of Mary.

But something good came out of all this scheming. This fanatical woman had helped to open people's eyes to the tricks and false miracles which the religious orders used — and so prepared the way for the fall of the monasteries.

9. Bishop of Worcester

1534 – 1535

As the new year dawned in 1534 Latimer looked back over the past. The previous year had brought frustration, difficulties and danger, and the year before that he had been forced to go to London to be tried by Convocation and had barely escaped with his life. Now the future appeared much brighter. A pang went through his heart as he thought of Bilney's death, and the words of Bainham on the night before his martyrdom echoed through his mind: 'I exhort you to stand to the defence of the truth.' Cranmer and he, together with the other Reformers, were doing this. Two years previously supporters for the Reformation had seemed few, but now they were steadily increasing in numbers. Since the new act of Parliament the powers of the bishops had become severely restricted. Henry's experience with the papacy and his gratitude to his Protestant subjects for bringing to light the conspiracy against him, led the Reformers to hope that he would be generous in lending his power to support more drastic reforms in the church.

For the last ten years Latimer had known little else than controversy and disappointment, both of which had dogged him since his conversion. It now looked as if he were entering a new era, but how long would it last? Latimer wondered if the king would ever invite him to preach again. He had not preached before Henry since the false charges levelled against him at Bristol. But Cranmer had not forgotten this either and before long Latimer received a letter from him. Cranmer had found an opportunity to ask the king if Latimer could preach at the court in Lent, and Henry had agreed. Cranmer told Latimer with delight that the final seal had been set on his return to royal favour. But Cranmer also warned Latimer in his letter that he must be discreet in his choice of words. Some of the old, blunt expressions that he had used in the past had been overlooked at the time, but if he used them now he might annoy Henry. Expressions used in his country church and among Bristol merchants would not do in court, so Cranmer urged caution in the language used.

When Cranmer received the king's permission, he advised the Dean of the Chapel Royal that Latimer was to preach at the king's request. Sampson, the Dean of the Chapel Royal, had been a member of the Convocation that had condemned Latimer. It was a bitter pill for him to swallow when he learnt that the man whom he had declared a heretic would officiate as court preacher for Lent. 'I favour him in my mind for his learning,' wrote the dean, 'I pray God it may be moderate (the times are most unpleasant), since that his teaching moveth no little dissension among the people wheresoever he cometh, the which is either a token of new doctrine, or else negligence in not expressing of his mind more clearly to the people.' [1] So, with the worst possible grace, the dean agreed, and Latimer preached once a week from February to March, 1534.

There is no record of the subjects that he chose but after Cranmer's warning it is probable that his themes were selected after consultation with the archbishop. No angry controversy followed, so it would appear that his sermons, however bold and hard-hitting, were more carefully worded than on former occasions.

It was just as well that no dissension followed Latimer's sermons, since the 'Reformation Parliament', as it became known, was sitting and was about to take some of the boldest steps in its history. After the pope's reactions to the new Parliament and the discovery of the treason by the nun of Kent and her collaboration with Catherine and her partisans, Henry decided to take more drastic action. Parliament decreed that all appeals to Rome were now prohibited and bulls for the consecration of bishops were no longer to come

1. From the State Paper Office.

from the Bishop of Rome. They were to be elected by the
dean and chapter on royal recommendation. This was to
affect Latimer's future. All payments to Rome, all pensions
and everything that had been drained from the country in
money and clergy were to cease. The power and jurisdiction
that the pope had claimed was to be transferred to the king.
He took upon himself the authority to inspect all religious
houses and reform them. If anyone refused to accept the
king's orders he was liable to the penalty of *Praemunire*.[2] All
traces of papal supremacy were abolished. After many
centuries under the power of the pope, England was at last
free. She was like a man who had been tied to the ground
with rope after rope. As Parliament passed the laws which
broke the connection with Rome, one rope after another was
cut until the prisoner escaped from bondage.

The clergy were powerless to prevent these changes. Their
spirit and power were broken and they lacked the courage to
make a united opposition to Henry. Most of them were
furious but they had to pretend that they submitted to his
new laws. Convocation had an even more painful task to perform: it had to pass acts to terminate its own authority. This
was nothing less than official suicide. The vital question to be
debated and decided was 'whether the Bishop of Rome had,
by Scripture, any more jurisdiction within the realm of
England than any other foreign bishop'. This question went
to the root of all the papal claims and, whether they realized
it or not, this was the scriptural test. A large majority decided
that the papal claims were false — only four people in the
Lower House were bold enough to vote in favour of the
papacy.

None of this was done out of zeal for the Reformers but,
as one writer has said, 'The legislation of Parliament was as
prompt and decisive as the boldest Reformer could have
wished.' Parliament and Convocation agreed to abolish all
traces of papal supremacy in England and throw off this yoke
of ignorance and tyranny. This was partly due to the growing

2. See chapter 6, page 46.

light and freedom of the age of the Renaissance. While this helped the Reformers in many ways, Parliament solemnly protested that their proceedings were not to be interpreted as if 'the king and his subjects intended to decline, or vary from the congregation of Christ's church in any things concerning the very articles of the catholic faith of Christendom'.[3] Parliament had no intention of varying its doctrine in any way. England was to be 'popish without acknowledging the pope', and to adhere to the teachings of Rome in past centuries.

Nevertheless, from the outset Parliament partly relaxed the cruel laws which had permitted persecution of the Reformers. It was no longer heresy to speak against the Bishop of Rome and his pretended authority. People accused of heresy were to be tried in an open court instead of secretly, as before. They could be released on bail and, if they were found guilty and they refused to abjure, they could not be burnt without a royal writ. The arbitrary violence of the ecclesiastical courts was abolished and people who had long been imprisoned on suspicion of heresy were set free.

Another important act was also passed at this time, which limited the succession to the throne of Henry's children to those by Anne who, it declared, was 'his lawful wife'. To say or do anything to the slander of Henry's marriage to Anne was treason and everyone had to take a solemn oath to observe the succession. This act was passed on 23 March 1534, and it is ironic that on the same day Clement VII, after seven years' hesitation, decided on his final sentence and solemnly declared that Henry's marriage to Catherine was valid. He ordered Henry to receive her again as his wife. The pope died soon after he had arrived at this decision and pious Christians saw God's hand at work. They realized that if Clement had died two years earlier, the new pontiff might have given Henry a divorce, these acts would never had been passed, and England would still be bound to the see of Rome.

At last English law was supreme over all people in England,

3. *Statutes of the Realm*, 25 Henry VIII.

clergy and laymen alike. The Church of England was freed from the old allegiance to Rome but bound to the throne instead. The tables had been turned on the clergy. For centuries they had known one master, the pope, and they had persecuted and imprisoned people with impunity. Now they had a new master and, as they felt the hand of the king upon them, they had to make the choice betwen perjury and treason. As one historian, Demaus, records, 'It was not yet a reformation, for Parliament had not formally adopted any of the doctrinal tenets of the Reformers; but it was a revolution.'

While many of the clergy were cowed by the king's action, some were willing to face death rather than perjure their consciences, and others waited and hoped to regain the lost power at a later date. Religious orders expressed their anger and dissatisfaction as boldly as they dared. Henry was aware of the smouldering discontent and knew that it could break out and become a raging fire, but circumstances — and his own will — had forced him to take this line. Once he decided on his course, he pursued it without hesitation despite the grumbles and danger of opposition.

Henry had not yet finished with the church. When Parliament reassembled in November the famous Act of Supremacy was passed. It declared that the king was 'the only supreme head in earth of the Church of England', and that he had 'full power and authority' to deal with reform, heresy, errors and abuses. If any person attempted to deprive the king of his spiritual dignity or title, or to call him a heretic, schismatic or infidel, they would be guilty of high treason. The church had become a department of state.

Although Henry is credited with most of these actions, his right-hand man and adviser was Thomas Cromwell, and he, more than anyone else, was responsible for the king's actions. Cranmer records that: 'Cromwell had done more than all others together in whatever was effected respecting the reformation of religion and the clergy.'[4] Cromwell had a definite aim, but so far he had failed to find anyone other

4. *Original Letters*, Parker Society, p. 15.

than Cranmer who would co-operate with him. When he eventually met Latimer he found in him a man who shared the same views, ideals and objectives. Cromwell recognized that Latimer was a person of power and ability, whose zeal and eloquence could move the mind of the nation. His skill in preaching would support the policy the king had chosen. The two men drew closer together and a deep friendship developed. Latimer was too honest to be a mere tool of any statesman and he had no great ambitions, but he assisted Cromwell because he agreed with him and was therefore able to assert his own convictions. He zealously promoted Cromwell's policy since he saw that it would remove the gross abuses in the church against which he preached.

Cromwell needed a friend who was a priest because he faced a difficult opponent — the church. The church had become stubborn and, while it had yielded to the acts of Parliament, it still made full use of its own secret weapon, the confessional. Treasonable words were whispered in the confessional into the ears of loyal subjects, and the hierarchy made full use of this Romanist instrument to spread its anger at Henry's legislation throughout the length of the country.

But Henry and Cromwell were prepared. They had no intention of allowing the clergy to criticize their policy or their actions. They expected them as a body to be hostile and knew that their preaching could influence the minds of the people, so all licences to preach were withdrawn and those who held them appeared before the bishops and were warned not to speak of any matters that touched the king, his laws or the succession. Any preacher who was suspected of being troublesome was refused the renewal of his licence.

In June 1534, a proclamation appeared which commanded bishops and clergy to preach every Sunday and to emphasize that the king alone was the head of the church, and ordered that all prayers and rubrics in the service books, where the Bishop of Rome was named, must be erased. As a double check Henry ordered his loyal subjects to see whether the clergy obeyed this proclamation. In other words, the people were to act as spies on the clergy. The magistrates and justices of the peace had similar instructions and the whole country was placed on its guard for, despite his success, Henry knew he was on dangerous ground and could omit no precaution.

There were two notable exceptions to those who conformed, namely Sir Thomas More and Bishop Fisher. Both refused to take the Oath of Succession as passed by Parliament. They were willing to swear to the succession but only in a modified form, since they objected to certain expressions. Cranmer entreated that they might be permitted to take it in this modified form but Parliament refused to allow this, so Henry had no alternative but to imprison them. It is interesting to note that this was the only time that More's and Latimer's paths crossed. More had been summoned to Lambeth to the commissioners, while Cranmer tried to persuade him to take the oath. While the commissioners were discussing More he was asked to go into the palace garden. He records in a letter to his daughter that while he was waiting he saw 'Master Doctor Latimer come into the garden; and there walked he with divers other doctors and chaplains of my lord of Canterbury'. In two years the pendulum had swung the other way: two years ago Latimer had thought of flight to the Continent while More was Lord Chancellor; now More sensed that his head was not secure on his shoulders, while Latimer gained royal favour. A new day was dawning for England.

In 1535 neither Parliament nor Convocation assembled; it was a year of stern action with no time for debate. Henry had marked out the path for all his subjects and refused to allow anyone to turn to right or left. Those who denied the royal supremacy or the Oath of Succession could be hanged and quartered for high treason. Henry struck out in all directions. In May 1535 fourteen Dutch Anabaptists were burned at Smithfield for heresy; in June three monks of Charter House were hanged as traitors still wearing their priestly vestments as a warning to other clergy. More and Fisher both remained true to their faith and after a year in jail they followed those who had already laid down their lives.

Fisher, whose learning and high character had made him leader of the ecclesiastics in England and who supported the pope, had been imprisoned for his part in the imposture of the nun of Kent. He was tried for denying Henry the title of 'Supreme head in earth of the Church of England' and was condemned and beheaded on 22 June 1535. He died calmly and bravely. Two weeks later, Sir Thomas More followed him to the block. He was condemned and executed for the same offence. More was recognized as 'a man of incomparable genius' (Erasmus), a man of wit and learning and, while there was much cruelty in his nature, his courage and determination to stand by what he believed were qualities to be admired. Nevertheless, while his courage is praiseworthy, it must be recorded that some of the actions of this great lawyer and Chancellor of England were not ethical by the legal standards of any era: he sanctioned the imprisonment and death of a number of English subjects in circumstances which were contrary to English law.

By putting More and Fisher to death, Henry threw down the gauntlet to the pope. The pontiff lost no time in replying to this rebellious son of the church. On 30 August 1535, he issued a bull against Henry depriving him of his dominions, absolving his subjects from their allegiance, and placing the kingdom under an interdict. The pope then urged all orthodox sovereigns to unite in a crusade against him. But Henry, on his part, was prepared and he knew where most support for the pope would come from — the clergy quartered in the papal garrisons and in the monastic houses that existed in every county. If the pope had made his plans, the king had also made his.

* * * * * * *

Not only had Henry frequently expressed his keenness for Latimer's preaching, but Queen Anne also longed to hear him preach and teach. She had loved his sermons from the day she first heard him and he remained a special favourite with her.

It is notable that a change appears to have come over Anne after she ascended the throne. Before she became queen she was ambitious and worldly, but afterwards she wished to be a spiritual mother to her people and give them the Word of God through the best preachers that the country possessed. When she learned from Cromwell of merchants who had suffered for having smuggled Tyndale's New Testament into England, she ordered him to repay the merchants. It soon became known to the people that Anne was keen for the New Testament to be read and that she wished to help those who favoured the Reformation. Instead of going to Cromwell, some who had lost their goods for smuggling in the New Testament went straight to the queen. While Anne's actions were highly commendable and suggest a real change of heart, they were not diplomatic and they did not pass unnoticed by the king, who became intensely jealous.

In 1534 Tyndale, still a refugee and hunted from one town to another on the Continent, expressed his gratitude to the queen. He sent her a large de luxe copy of the New Testament, printed on vellum with gilt edges. This volume is preserved in the British Library and is a monument to the veneration that Tyndale had for Anne Boleyn. But Anne attempted to influence Henry and this sowed seeds of suspicion in his mind. He was quick to notice when a friend of Tyndale's, a merchant named Harman who had brought many of his books into England, was declared by Anne to be a 'good Christian'. She dared to profess herself a friend of this heretic whom Henry hated! He said nothing at the time but stored these things up in his heart, and Anne failed to perceive that her faithfulness to the gospel that she was beginning to love was jeopardizing her position as Henry's wife.

Doctrinally Henry had not changed his position. At the end of 1534 he issued a prohibition of suspected books. Convocation had persuaded him to take this step and its main object was to ban Tyndale's translation. That faithful Reformer now lived in Antwerp so that he might be as near as possible to the ships that carried his books to England. That year he completed a revision of his New Testament and Queen

Anne's copy was a sample of it. Ninety per cent of the New Testament of the King James Version of the Bible came from this translation.

In the summer of 1535 a renegade young Englishman, Henry Phillips — who had a fanatical hatred for the king and the Reformers — played the part of Judas and, for a bribe from the Roman hierarchy, obtained the services of the Emperor Charles's attorney and then went to Antwerp. He had already made friends with Tyndale and with Thomas Poyntz, the merchant who was Tyndale's host. He led Tyndale into a trap, as a result of which the Reformer was thrown into a dungeon in the castle of Vilvorde, just outside Brussels. The man who had supplied England with the Word of God, which frees men from the slavery of sin and of Rome, had now become a prisoner himself.

* * * * * * *

Gifted preachers were so few at this time that Latimer probably spent much of his time in the West of England, preaching in towns and villages near to his country parish. It is also highly probable that he preached in London in the spring of 1535 since, at a time when the acts of Parliament caused so much hostility, the voice of a gifted and eloquent preacher could do much to quieten the people. During the summer he spent much time in London discussing matters with Cranmer and Cromwell. Cranmer was almost the only leading clergyman in favour of the Reformation and was anxious that Latimer should be elevated to one of the vacant bishoprics. He would then have a friend and supporter in Convocation. Cromwell, for his part, was equally keen to see Latimer on the bench and to avail himself of his shrewd advice. Latimer and Nicholas Shaxton had for several years been conspicuous for their zeal in defending Henry's cause and these two were destined for the vacant sees of Worcester and Salisbury.

Latimer bore no trace of selfish ambition. He coveted neither wealth nor power, but whenever he saw an opportunity to reform the church and advance the reading and exposition of the Bible he would take it. He knew the work would be hard and uphill and he was no longer a young man, but he remained undaunted. At that time Worcester had an Italian bishop, Ghinucci, who had never been in England. For forty years Worcester and Salisbury had been governed by a succession of Italian prelates, not one of whom ever visited his bishopric. Parliament deprived them of their sees, which it declared vacant in 1534. It gave the absent bishops four months to come and claim their dioceses, provided they would also take an oath to observe the laws of England. This they failed to do, so, in May 1535, Nicholas Shaxton was appointed Bishop of Salisbury and on 12 August 1535, the royal assent was given to the appointment of Latimer as Bishop of Worcester.

Two and a half years previously he had faced the bishops as an accused heretic. Now he was to sit with them and, apart from Cranmer and Shaxton, they were either hostile or, at best, indifferent to reform. What did the future hold in store for him in this new role and in these circumstances?

10. Visitation of monasteries

1535 – May 1536

Upon his appointment as Bishop of Worcester Latimer found that he had oversight of a great many churches, yet the curious thing was that there were also many religious houses — monasteries and convents — over which he had no oversight or control. Each of these had its own abbot, prior or mother superior who was directly responsible to the pope. This state of affairs had long been the grievance of many bishops, who objected to the fact that there were several clergy in their diocese whom they were unable to discipline since they took their orders from the pope alone.

Where did these monasteries and convents come from and why were they formed? One of the best authorities on this subject says, 'In order to understand the Roman Catholic position regarding the grouping of men and women in monasteries and convents we must understand the basic viewpoint which underlies that system. During the Middle Ages the idea developed in Roman theology that man's work was to be divided into the natural (i.e. the secular) and the spiritual. Only the spiritual was thought to be pleasing to God. Consequently, while the natural man might be satisfied with the common virtues of daily life, the ideal was that of the mystic who in deep contemplation reached out for the spiritual. In achieving this higher life the natural was thought of not as a help but as a hindrance. The life of the monk and the nun who withdrew from society and from the workaday life of the world and retired into the quiet of the cloisters, thus losing themselves in mystic contemplation, was thought to be the higher life. There, in seclusion from the world, the image of God which had been lost in the Fall, was to be restored in its beauty. The monastic system is thus based on two false

Worcester Cathedral. (Reproduced by courtesy of Barnaby's Picture Library.)

principles, namely, that celibacy is a holier state than matrimony, and that total withdrawal from the social intercourse and business life of the world is conducive to true religion.'[1]

This idea was not new since it had long been present in the East and had been strongly developed in Buddhism, which had monks and nuns long before the Christian church was founded. The practice of withdrawing from society appears to have originated in Egypt in about the third century A.D., when various hermits withdrew into the desert and, after a short time, a group of followers gathered round these hermits, who were regarded as saints. Originally the movement was confined to Egypt, then it spread to Palestine, Syria and Asia Minor in the fourth century and from there into Europe. Later, various leaders drew up codes for those who wished to enter their order when they established a monastery or convent, and this policy spread throughout Christendom.

In the twelfth century the friars, the preaching orders, were founded. They took the same vows of celibacy, poverty, chastity and obedience when they entered their order. These monks, nuns and friars were regarded as outstanding Christians by ordinary folk. This was based mainly on the idea that matter was evil and that there was something unclean about marriage and sex. Therefore, the less a person had to do with the world and those of the opposite sex, the holier his life could be.

Latimer says in one of his letters, 'I have thought in times past that if I had been a friar and in a cowl, I could not have been damned nor afraid of death; and by reason of the same I have been minded many times to have been a friar, namely, when I was sore sick or diseased. Now I abhor my superstitious foolishness.' His words describe the view held by most people: even a bishop like himself was considered inferior to those shut away in the cloisters. To the average person it seemed a passport to heaven to enter a religious order. But

1. L. Boettner, *Roman Catholicism*, Presbyterian and Reformed Publishing Co. 1962, pp. 300-301.

what was the actual state of the monasteries at this time, and were the inmates as holy as was generally believed?

When Luther heard that Henry had abolished the power of the pope in England but left the monasteries untouched, he smiled. 'The King of England weakens the body of the papacy but at the same time strengthens the soul!' he said. Cromwell shared Luther's view and by now he had risen high in the king's favour. 'The papacy and monasteries must stand or fall together,' he declared. 'Sire, the most fanatical enemies of your supreme authority are to be found in the religious houses,' he told Henry. After abolishing the power of the pope Cromwell realized that the monasteries, too, must be done away with. One of the factors that precipitated this was the immorality of the monks and nuns.

Rumours soon spread round the court that Henry proposed to interfere with the religious houses, and friends of the papacy were horrified. 'These foundations were consecrated to Almighty God,' one courtier maintained, 'respect therefore those retreats where pious souls live in contemplation.' 'Contemplation!' Sir Henry Colt replied scornfully. 'Tomorrow, Sire, I undertake to produce proofs of the kind of contemplation in which these monks indulge.' One old historian records that Colt knew that a number of monks of Waltham Abbey liked to pass the night with the nuns of Chesham Convent, so he went to a narrow path through which the monks passed on their way to the abbey and stretched across it a stout net, as used in stag-hunting. About daybreak, as the monks returned with their lanterns in their hands they heard a loud trumpet blast from one of Colt's men. They blew out their lanterns in alarm and hurried away, only to fall into the trap laid for them. The next day Colt presented them to the king who laughed heartily. 'I have often seen better game,' he said, 'but never fatter . . . I can make a better use of the money which the monks waste on their debaucheries. The coast of England requires to be fortified, my fleet and army to be increased . . . All that is well worth the trouble of suppressing houses of impurity.'

As one Victorian writer, Ryle, says, 'Take any number of

men and women, of any nation, rank or class, bind them by
a vow of celibacy, shut them up in houses by themselves, give
them plenty to eat and drink, and give them nothing to do,
and above all, give them no Bible reading, no true religion,
no preaching of the gospel, no inspection, and no check from
public opinion; if the result of all this be not abominable and
abundant breach of the seventh commandment, I can only
say that I have read human nature in vain.'

Latimer, meantime, had settled down in his new diocese
but found the work hard. To a man of his zeal it was difficult
to deal with the ignorant and superstitious clergy that came
under him. He also had to walk carefully since he was aware
of Henry's reluctance to permit any wide departure from the
doctrine and ritual to which he was firmly attached. Wherever he could, he pressed on with the work of reforming his
diocese and instructing his clergy with scriptural teaching.
But he was powerless to touch the abbeys and convents, none
of which would acknowledge his authority as bishop.

Latimer was delighted when he received a letter from
Cranmer. It stated that the king had decided to order a
general visitation of the monasteries so as to determine what
should be done when the visitation was completed. Cromwell
was to take charge of this and Henry had made him his vicar-
general with all the ecclesiastical authority of the king. He
was instructed to visit all churches and monasteries of both
men and women: 'You will correct and punish whoever may
be found guilty,' the king said, and the visitation began in
September 1535.

When the news reached the monks and nuns they trembled
with fright. Faith in their orders no longer existed, the
confidence they once had in monastic practices, relics and
pilgrimages had grown weak. They knew that when the commissioners arrived the truth would be revealed. Cromwell
gave his commissioners their instructions, the questions they
were to put to the monks, the orders they were to give to
the abbots and priors, and then sent them on their way. The
universities were not overlooked, since they, too, badly
needed reform. The Royal Commissioners were ordered to

visit Oxford and Cambridge and report on the state of the colleges.

Latimer was eager for more news but after Christmas 1535 he was no longer dependent on Cranmer's letters. As a bishop he was entitled to sit in the House of Lords as one of the 'lords spiritual', so he was present when the commissioners returned to London and laid their report before Parliament early in 1536. Throughout the autumn of 1535 they had been inspecting all the smaller religious houses, and both Lords and Commons waited eagerly to hear what they had to say. Latimer was horrified as he leaned back in his seat and listened to the report; it was far worse than he had feared. 'We have discovered not seven, but more than seven hundred thousand deadly sins,' they asserted. 'Here are the confessions of the monks and nuns subscribed with their own hands. . . . The monasteries are so full of iniquity that they ought to fall down under such a weight. If there be here and there any innocent cloisters, they are so few in number that they cannot save the others.'

The visitation had begun with the smaller houses in Canterbury and these monasteries disclosed immorality of the worst order. The commissioners took their seats in one of the halls of the Augustinian monastery and the monks came before them, some embarrassed, others bold, but most of them careless. They were then questioned: 'Are there any among you who disguising themselves, leave the convent and go vagabondizing about?' asked the commissioners. 'Do you observe the vow of chastity, and has anyone been convicted of incontinence? Do women enter the monastery or live in it habitually?' The answers to these questions were scandalous. Eight of the monks were convicted of abominable vices and set aside for punishment.

Some historians have assumed that there was haste and exaggeration on the part of the visitors, but when allowance is made for the flowery language used, recent historians have agreed that basically the facts laid before Parliament were not exaggerated. The book containing the commissioners' report became known as the *Black Book* because it recorded all the

misdeeds of the religious orders, and Cromwell had it read to
the House. Unfortunately it no longer exists; it is believed that
it was destroyed in the reign of the ardent Catholic Queen
Mary, who did not wish this record to be preserved. The facts
were clearly recorded and the confessions of monks and nuns
signed by their own hands were shown to Parliament. Uproar
broke out immediately. 'Down with their houses!' the
members shouted. 'Suppress them!' roared others.

In spite of this the members were generally interested in the
preservation of the houses. Most had some connection with
one cloister or another, and several had friends and relations
who were in one of the orders. Nevertheless the condemnation
was general. Convocation and provincial councils had attempted to reform these monasteries for several centuries but
without success. Now they were to fall under the hand of the
secular power because they had become so corrupt.

It is interesting to note that when the visitors came to the
houses it was like a cup of joy to many of the inmates. Most
of them were placed there in their childhood and detained
against their will. According to Cromwell's orders, no one
was to be forced to stay. They were told that every monk
under twenty-four years of age and every nun under twenty-
one might go free. Almost all seized this opportunity to
escape. They were supplied with clothes and money and
departed rejoicing, while older monks and nuns fell on their
knees and begged the commissioners to obtain the same
favour for them.

It is pleasant to record that in a few places the commissioners found that the monks were living a holy life in accor-
dance with the vows they had taken. The commissioners
praised them in their report and asked the king to preserve
these monasteries.

Naturally, the king and Parliament were greatly interested
in the income which flowed into these houses. The members
were amazed when they learnt how much money poured into
the coffers of these idle men and women. 'We must, above all
things, diminish the wealth of the clergy,' Dr. Cox said, 'for
so long as they do not imitate the poverty of Christ, the

people will not follow their teaching. I have no doubt,' he added with a touch of irony, 'that the bishops, priests and monks will readily free themselves from the heavy burden of wealth of every kind, which renders the fulfilment of their spiritual duties impossible.'

'The heavy burden of wealth' to which Dr Cox referred is estimated by a recent historian to have been about £163,000 per annum, while the annual income of the government was slightly more than £100,000. This alone shows how they could live in such luxury and explains why the king and the nobles were anxious to do away with them and lay their hands on the wealth. These were men and women who on entering their monastery took a vow of poverty!

Apart from Latimer's natural interest in the state of the monasteries, as Bishop of Worcester he was particularly concerned because of the large number that lay in his diocese. The diocese of Worcester was much more extensive then and stretched beyond Bristol. Many of the offending monasteries in the *Black Book* lay in Latimer's diocese.

While there was this loud cry in Parliament for the dissolution of the monasteries, it must be noted that the large monasteries were less disorderly than the smaller ones and Cromwell limited himself to the suppression of three hundred and seventy-two smaller cloisters. The abbots of the larger ones, flattered by this exception made to them, were silent and hoped that they would escape — but in fact they had only been given a reprieve. 'These monasteries,' Cromwell said, 'being the dishonour of religion, and all the attempts, repeated through more than two centuries, having shown that their reformation is impossible, the king, as supreme head of the church, under God, proposes to the Lords and Commons, and these agree, that the possessions of the said houses shall cease to be wasted for the maintenance of sin, and shall be converted to better uses.'

When the news spread throughout England that the monasteries were to be destroyed a great uproar broke out. Superstition became active and feeble minds believed all that was told them. 'The Virgin has appeared to certain monks,' some said, 'and ordered them to serve her as they had hitherto done.' 'What! No more religious houses?' others exclaimed through their tears. Latimer had his answer ready. 'On the contrary,' he said, 'look at that man and woman living together piously, tranquilly, in the fear of God, keeping His Word and active in the duties of their calling: they form a religious house, one that is truly acceptable to God. Pure religion consists not in wearing a hood, but in visiting the fatherless and the widows, and keeping ourselves unspotted from the world. What has hitherto been called a religious life was an unreligious life; yea, rather an hypocrisy.'

But while Latimer gave his voice and support to dealing with vice and corruption, he was opposed to spoiling the monasteries and allowing the nobles and king to grasp their wealth. He was the only one among the few evangelicals who raised his voice in favour of the religious bodies. He was anxious that a few monasteries should be preserved as houses of prayer, study, hospitality and, above all, preaching. He knew well that England desperately needed preachers, and preachers must be trained. If Latimer's voice had only been heeded, how different our history might have been.

On 11 March 1536, the bill for the smaller houses passed through the Commons and the wealth of the monasteries was taken by the Crown. Apart from the greed shown by the king and nobles, other evils must be recorded. Some of the finest libraries in England were destroyed and works of great value were sold for a trifle, many to people on the Continent. All the land held by the monasteries passed into the hands of the nobility. This was another evil that Latimer had feared for, despite the wealth and idle lives of the monks, the tenants had received fair treatment from the abbots. When the nobles became landlords they received much harsher treatment.

It is only right to record that the monks were treated fairly, since they each received a pension in proportion to their age and those who wished to continue as monks were sent to the larger monasteries. But the young ones, under twenty-five, were told that they must work for their living and the same rule was applied to the nuns. This caused much suffering since they had never worked in the real sense of the word. Many had entered the cloisters as children and were untrained in any manual skills. Soon they could be seen going from door to door begging and asking for shelter for the night.

Another danger arose when the greedy eyes of the nobles also fell on Oxford and Cambridge. Were these two seats of learning to fall? England was in peril of losing her universities, but when Henry remembered the days of his youth and the lectures given by Erasmus at Oxford, he stepped in before anything could be touched. 'I will not permit the wolves around me to fall upon the universities,' he declared. All his life Henry remained a lover of art and learning. In fact some of the wealth of the monasteries was used to found new colleges and to assist others, especially Trinity College, Cambridge. These institutions helped to spread the light of the Renaissance and of the Reformation throughout England. Latimer's gratitude to Henry for his intervention was most marked as he, too, recalled the days he had spent at Cambridge as student and lecturer, and it was there that the light of God's Word had first come to him.

11. 'Fornicators and adulterers God will judge'

Although Latimer was now Bishop of Worcester he spent some of his time away from his diocese. He was often in court and one of the people who had the greatest admiration for him and his preaching was the queen. From the first day that Anne Boleyn met Latimer, the simplicity of his style of preaching moved her and she loved listening to him. Enthusiasm for Latimer was widespread. 'It is as impossible for us to receive into our minds all the treasures of eloquence and knowledge which fall from his lips, as it would be for a little river to contain the waters of the ocean in its bed,' his hearers said.

From the time that he preached the Lent sermons before the king in 1535, Latimer was one of Anne's favourites and he had a definite influence upon her. Although we have referred to the interest and concern that the queen showed in the Protestant cause, it appears doubtful if she had as yet experienced that inner working of the Holy Spirit that men like Bilney, Latimer, Tyndale and Cranmer knew. She was a good wife and a good Protestant — strongly attached to Scripture and opposed to the pope, but she still lacked true spiritual awakening. Indeed, it might well be said that, as queen and wife of Henry, her very position hindered her from making spiritual progress. But since she came to the throne Anne appears to have taken a greater interest in the things of God. She was in frequent contact with Cranmer, too, as she was concerned about the need for Christian preachers.

Anne also interested herself in finding suitable students for Oxford and Cambridge. She looked for young men with pure morals and clear intellects who were keen to support the Protestant cause. She was careful and required testimonials certifying the purity of morals and intellectual ability of prospective students. When she was satisfied she placed them at one of the universities and asked them, while they studied, to spread the New Testament and the writings of the Reformers. Many of these men did much service to both church and state.

About this time Anne lost one of her chaplains, Dr Betts, and looked for a godly man to take his place. She met Matthew Parker, a Fellow of Corpus Christi College, Cambridge, who had faithfully preached the gospel for several years. When Parker heard that Anne wanted him to become chaplain he was amazed and nervous at such an honour, but Latimer wrote to him, 'Show yourself to the world; hide yourself no longer; work good while it is day, the night comes when no man can work. We know what you can do; let not your will be less than your power.' So Parker went to court and gained the esteem of the queen through his knowledge, piety and prudence. Anne's liveliness and gaiety were in strong contrast to the graver and stiffer formalities of the English ladies in court. Latimer had frequently admonished her respectfully when they were alone and Anne would always exclaim with gratitude, 'You do me so much good! Pray never pass over a single fault.'

While the Protestant cause was making slow but steady progress, the enemies of the Reformers could not forget the recent wounds that had been inflicted on the papacy or the monasteries it had lost. In return, one person must be laid on the altar and sacrificed, one taken from the highest possible station. In the eyes of the Catholics, Anne had committed an unpardonable sin — she had caused England to be separated from Rome. In order to marry her, Henry had needed a divorce and had obtained that divorce only by separating himself from the church and from Rome. The Catholics' hatred for her knew no bounds and they were determined to destroy her. Unknown to her, Anne Boleyn's star was already setting.

Anne's uncle, the proud Duke of Norfolk, was one of the leaders of the papal party and he nursed a secret but burning animosity towards this young woman who had become queen and who supported the Reformers. Anne's father, the Earl of Wiltshire, felt that Henry was not flattered at becoming his son-in-law and decided that, since he was now out of favour with the king, he would leave London.

Anne had many enemies at court; she was to prove that it is rarely possible to climb high in this world without making foes. One of her maids of honour was Jane Seymour, who had all the attractions of youth and beauty, while her disposition struck a happy medium between the severity of Catherine and the fascinating vivacity of Anne. Henry's heart was easily inflamed and he soon became aware of Jane's graces and charms, while the charms of Anne Boleyn — which had once so captivated him — now repelled him. Henry had begun to show his real nature. The gaiety of the queen fatigued him and the zeal she showed for the Protestant cause alienated him. Anne's enemies were quick to notice this and resolved to take advantage of it to ruin her as soon as an opportunity arose.

Anne was misunderstood: her gaiety would have been quite natural had she been in France, but in England her behaviour caused some of the ladies of the court to suspect her of being a flirt, like many of them. Henry began to indulge in suspicions and Lady Rochford, an old enemy of Anne, was only too eager to feed his jealousy by crafty insinuations.

It was not long before Anne noticed the king's favour for Jane Seymour. As she watched her maid of honour, her pride was hurt and jealousy tortured her. She now knew what Catherine had suffered when she had watched Anne growing in favour in her husband's eyes. She tried to win back the king's love but Henry grew more angry with Anne every hour. Unfortunately, the queen was near her confinement and at the very moment when she hoped to give Henry the son for whom he longed, he withdrew from her completely. Anne's heart was almost broken and she wondered just what fate held in store for her.

Meanwhile Jane Seymour accepted the king's advances and a number of historians record that, at the end of January 1536, Anne unexpectedly entered a room in the palace and found Henry paying court to Jane in a very marked manner. It was as if a sword had pierced Anne's heart. She could not bear such a cruel blow and prematurely gave birth to a dead son. God had granted Henry his long-desired heir but the grief of the mother at the father's sin cost the child's life.

For some time Anne's life was despaired of and when Henry upbraided her for his misfortune, she could not restrain herself: 'You have no one to blame but yourself,' she cried. Henry answered her harshly and left the room. Anne recovered and again took her place in court but she seemed to foresee the misfortune that lay ahead of her. All attempts to regain Henry's affection were useless and her nights became disturbed by terrifying dreams.

Everyone observed the change and ardent Catholics regained their courage. Jane had natural allies at court and her two brothers, Edward and Thomas, both thought that a Seymour was as good as a Boleyn to wear the crown. As the Roman Catholic party sought to bring down Anne we need to remember that they had an instrument that could be used throughout the land to spread sedition as well as obtain secrets from people. This was the confessional. One ex-Catholic describes it as the 'system of espionage, the system of slavery. The priest is the spy in every home.' The confessional is the method whereby the Roman Catholic believes he obtains absolution for his sins as he goes weekly or monthly to confess to the priest all sins he has committed. But while Rome claims that it is for the purpose of confessing sins and gaining absolution from the priest, the confessional can also be used the other way round. Long before the telephone was invented, words whispered by the priest to the penitent under the 'seal of the confessional' could rapidly spread ugly rumours or poison people's minds throughout a parish, village or town. If this was done throughout the land, the slanderous or treasonable idea of some bishop could speedily be planted in the minds of the people without king or courtier being aware of what was taking place. It is highly probable that the confessional was used in this way to poison people's minds against Anne at this time.

* * * * * * *

Meanwhile, in Worcester, Latimer continued his work in his new diocese. There had been some delay in obtaining the necessary writ from Henry giving him the see. Latimer's health was also somewhat precarious and he had many invitations to preach. So, although we have little information of his activities in the autumn of 1535, we can be sure that he devoted all his time and energy to the work of ruling and reforming a diocese long accustomed to the licence of uncontrolled freedom where monks and priests had ruled supreme in ignorance and superstition.

When Christmas came Latimer, who had always observed it according to old English custom, loved to show benevolence to the poor. It was also customary for the people and clergy to give presents to their bishop on New Year's day in token of their esteem. Likewise the bishops and abbots were expected to give a New Year's gift to the king. Some of these presents consisted of enormous sums of money: richer bishops gave as much as £750, and the great abbey of Westminster gave £900 as its gift to win Henry's favour. On this, Latimer's first New Year as a bishop, he gave the king a most unusual present — but this is best told by Foxe: 'There was then and remaineth still, an ancient custom received from the old Romans, that upon New Year's day, being the first day of January, every bishop with some handsome New Year's gift should gratify the king; so they did, some with gold, some with silver, some with a purse full of money, and some one thing, some another. But Master Latimer, being Bishop of Worcester then, among the rest, presented a New Testament for his New Year's gift, with a napkin having this posy [inscription] about it, *Fornicatores et adulteros judicabit Dominus* [fornicators and adulterers God will judge].' [1]

1. Foxe, *Acts and Monuments*, vol. vii, p. 517.

Henry's neglect of Anne Boleyn and his open preference for Jane Seymour had been the topic of gossip at court for some time. It had reached Latimer's ears and we can be sure that he alone possessed the courage openly to rebuke the vices of his king as sternly as John the Baptist rebuked Herod. Furthermore he used that hated translation of Tyndale's with which to do it. The very sight of his New Testament was calculated to rouse Henry to fury. There is no record of his reaction to Latimer's gift but God's sovereign hand was upon His servant protecting him from any anger the king might have had. Latimer appears to have been the only person who could say things like this to Henry and the king appears to have accepted the rebuke because he knew it to be the truth. Nevertheless he continued in his sinful course. Latimer was deeply concerned about Anne and knew how much she supported the Protestant cause, but as Bishop of Worcester he was not in London as frequently as he would have liked and much took place in his absence.

Events moved quickly. In January 1536 Catherine of Aragon died peacefully in her sleep at Kimbolton Castle, after protesting that she and no one else was Henry's true and lawful wife. Her death was an event of national importance as diplomats were filled with excitement and anticipated changes in Henry's policy. It was obvious that the king had felt the danger of his position by openly rejecting the papacy and not allying himself with other Protestant countries. He had isolated himself from the other sovereigns of Europe and it was also becoming increasingly clear that Anne Boleyn was no longer the supreme mistress of his heart. To the Catholics it looked as if it would be possible to remove Anne and bring about a reconciliation between Henry and the pope. It was rumoured that even the emperor was willing to be reconciled to Henry. Now that Catherine was dead it was easier for even the pope to offer some apology for the harsh steps taken in the long controversy over her. But Henry was not to be reconciled easily; he had tasted freedom from the papal power which had dominated everyone from prince to peasant. Purely as a matter of policy,

rather than from conviction, he was compelled to draw closer
to the position taken by the Reformers.

In February Parliament and Convocation reassembled and
Latimer took his seat among the Lords and heard the result
of the visitation of the monasteries. But when this session
ended on 14 April, Parliament was dissolved. It had sat for
nearly seven years, an exceptionally long time for a Tudor
Parliament. But England owes far more to this Parliament
than we can ever appreciate. When the members assembled,
as Froude says, 'They found England in dependency on a
foreign power; they left it a free nation.' They had abolished
spiritual bondage which had kept the souls of the people in
slavery and darkness. They had defied the pope and suppressed the monasteries. They had dealt firmly and ruthlessly
with distinguished defenders of papacy. It must be admitted
that they had not proceeded far with the reformation of
religion, but in establishing the supremacy of the Crown in
place of the old assumption of the infallibility of the pope,
they had laid a firm foundation on which the new building of
toleration and religious liberty was to arise.

When Parliament rose, Anne began to feel forebodings of
an early death and her most anxious thoughts were for her
daughter. She wondered what would become of Elizabeth
and she wanted her to be brought up in the knowledge of the
gospel. She sent for Matthew Parker to tell him of her fears
and wishes and then committed Elizabeth to him. Anne's
words sank deeply into his heart and, twenty-three years later
when Elizabeth became queen and raised him to be Archbishop of Canterbury, he declared that if he were not under
such obligations to her mother he would never have consented to serve Elizabeth in such a high office.

After giving Elizabeth to Parker, Anne felt a little more at
ease but events moved even faster. Various trumped-up
charges were brought against her to Henry and this time he
was not going to endure the wearisome business of divorce;
he preferred a much quicker method of disposal — the axe.
On returning from a joust Henry said to some of his ministers,
'Tomorrow morning you will take Rochford, Norris and

Weston to the Tower; you will then proceed to Greenwich, arrest the queen and put her in prison.' The next day, 1 May, Anne was arrested, accused of adultery and infidelity and taken to the Tower, where she was imprisoned in one of the rooms in which she slept before her coronation. This sadistic touch of Henry's brought back so many memories that she collapsed and burst into tears. While awaiting her trial, Anne was surrounded by Henry's spies, old enemies who had hated her for years. It was hoped that she would say something inadvertently, or in her nightmares, that would give the king some basis for the charges.

Cranmer was informed by letter of her arrest and was astounded when he learned that she had been charged with these crimes. 'What! The queen in prison! The queen an adulteress!' he exclaimed. A struggle took place in his heart; he knew how much he owed to Anne and all she had done to befriend the Protestant cause. He had loved her as a daughter and respected her as his sovereign and was unable to account for the king's behaviour. While Cranmer was a godly man, he showed excessive indulgence to Henry and bent like a willow in the wind beneath his hand. He wrote a letter to the king which has since become famous, or rather infamous, as it betrays his own state of mind — hopelessly divided between regard for Anne, horror of the crime alleged against her, fear that the charge was true and fear of Henry. The letter, as one writer says, 'evidently perplexed Cranmer to pen as much as it has perplexed historians to interpret it', since in the early part he praises Anne's virtues but then hastens to tone down his boldness by assuring the king that he is certain that Henry would not have taken such drastic steps unless he were certain of her crime.

Although justice was still groping its way out of the medieval darkness, people were nevertheless tried, and a trial demanded witnesses and evidence. But Cranmer accepted Anne's guilt before any trial took place. He deserved the condemnation of James 1:8: 'a double-minded man, unstable in all his ways'. This letter reveals the cowardice that appeared from time to time throughout his life.

The Tower of London in the time of Henry VIII. (Reproduced by courtesy of Barnaby's Picture Library.)

Latimer, as far as is known, was back in his diocese of Worcester and was unaware of what was taking place. History is silent regarding him. But Anne longed to see him or Cranmer. 'Oh, if God permitted me to have my bishops [Cranmer and Latimer], they would plead to the king for me!' she exclaimed, but her wish was refused.

On 12 May, Norris, Weston, Brereton and the court musician, Smeaton, were all tried, accused of adultery with the queen. The three noblemen firmly denied the charge and only the court musician confessed a crime which he hoped would give him a place in history. Norris, Weston and Brereton were condemned to be beheaded and the musician to be hanged.

Three days later, on 15 May, the queen was taken, with her brother Lord Rochford, before their peers to be tried in the great hall of the Tower, to which the Lord Mayor with a few alderman and citizens were admitted. It was obvious to Anne from the outset that the trial was a mere farce and the verdict already decided. She entered with dignity and, after gracefully greeting the court, took her seat in the chair given to her because of her weakness or her rank. She had no advocate, but the modesty of her face, the dignity of her manner and the inner peace which showed in the serenity of her looks moved even her enemies. While she had been waiting in the Tower, words from Latimer's sermons and passages that she had read in Tyndale's New Testament had come alive to Anne. As one who realized that she was poised on the brink of eternity, the teaching of Scripture had taken on a new meaning for her. While she had lived a faithful Protestant, there is little doubt that she faced death as a definite Christian.

It was said by some that the calmness and nobility of the queen's deportment made it appear that she came, not to be tried, but to receive the honours due to a sovereign. When the indictment was read Anne was charged with adultery, incest and conspiracy against the king's person. She held up her hand and pleaded 'not guilty'; she then refuted and tore to pieces the accusation brought against her. As she had an excellent wit every word that she spoke struck home. One eye-witness said that it was impossible to look at her or hear her and not declare her innocent.

Anne was declared guilty by her uncle, the Duke of Norfolk, and sentenced to be taken back to the Tower to be either 'burnt or beheaded, according to his Majesty's good pleasure'. Anne heard her sentence pronounced with calmness. She raised her eyes to heaven and cried out, 'O Father, O Creator! Thou who art the way, the truth, and the life, knowest that I have not deserved this death!' She then turned to her judges and declared her innocence but it was obvious that she was already prepared to die. It is here that her faith shines through for she said in her speech, 'Do not think that I say this in the hope of prolonging my life, for He who saveth from death has taught me how to die, and will strengthen my faith. . . and then afterwards I shall live in eternal peace and joy without end, where I will pray to God for the king, and for you my lords.'

The wisdom and eloquence of the queen's speech, aided by her beauty and the expression of her voice, moved the whole court. As it broke up the Lord Mayor turned to a friend and said, 'I can only observe one thing in this trial — the fixed resolution to get rid of the queen at any price.' This is also the verdict of posterity. Henry treated Anne as he had treated Wolsey: when he had finished with her he tossed her aside as a spoiled child treats his toys. It is said of Louis XIV that he had more mistresses than Henry had wives but at least he knew how to dispose of them without murdering them.

Now that Anne was sentenced, Henry took another step to speed up events. He annulled his marriage with her. Whether in anger or sheer stupidity, he failed to see that he was contradicting himself. If there was no lawful marriage, there could be no adultery and the sentence based on this crime was, *ipso facto*, null. Cranmer perhaps hoped that Anne's life would be saved if the marriage was annulled, so he called a court which declared the marriage to be 'utterly void and of none effect'.

Anne was completely prepared for her death. On 19 May she appeared about noon dressed in a robe of black damask and attended by four maids of honour. She walked slowly to the scaffold that had been erected on the green at the Tower. Her step was firm and her appearance calm as she approached the block on which she was to lay her head. The executioner, whom Henry had brought over from Calais, was there with his sword waiting. Before she died Anne spoke to those who had been her subjects: 'Good Christian people, I am not come here to justify myself; I leave my justification entirely to Christ, in whom I put my trust. I will accuse no man, nor speak anything of that whereof I am accused, as I know full well that aught that I could say in my defence doth not pertain unto you, and that I could draw no hope of life from the same. I come here only to die, according as I have been condemned. . . thus I take my leave of the world and of you, and heartily desire you all to pray for me. O Lord, have mercy upon me! To God I commit my soul!'

The queen removed her white collar and took off her hood that the sword might not be impeded, then she fell on her knees and prayed silently for a few moments. She moved closer to the block and laid her head on it. 'O Christ, into Thy hands I commit my soul!' she cried. The headsman, disturbed by the mildness of her face, hesitated for a few seconds until his courage returned. Anne cried again, 'O Jesus, receive my soul!' The sword flashed through the air and her head fell. A cry went up from the onlookers; it was as if they had received the blow on their own necks. Anne's words had moved even the hardest hearts there and her faith had shone through.

Henry was waiting in Epping Forest under an oak. A gunner at the Tower fired his gun as he saw Anne's head roll and this was relayed to Henry. When the cannon shot resounded the king rose up. 'Ha, ha! The deed is done!' he exclaimed. 'Uncouple the hounds and away.' On the same day, 19 May, Cranmer issued a special licence to enable Henry to marry Jane Seymour. The next day Henry and Jane were betrothed and, ten days later, were married at York Place. As

Demaus has said, 'Who has ever really doubted that Anne's execution was very like murder under form of law? ... Henry himself, indeed, has furnished the most unanswerable refutation of the pleas of his apologists. By marrying Jane Seymour. . . the day after Anne's execution, he has rendered it for ever impossible for any evidence to demonstrate his innocence.'

Anne was a power behind the Reformers. She encouraged them and they in turn helped her — Tyndale by his translation and Latimer by his sermons. It is impossible to segregate church and state in the Reformation. Both were used by God to bring about His plans and Queen Anne was one of the people used by Him to help the Reformers from a position of authority in the state. She died at twenty-nine years of age showing that her faith was real and that Latimer's preaching had fallen on good ground.

12. Latimer, voice of the people

May 1536 – January 1537

When the news of Anne's death and Henry's marriage to Jane Seymour reached Latimer he was grieved and greatly disturbed. He was sorrowful at the death of Anne, who had been not only his queen, but also his friend and a loyal supporter of the Reformers, and he was disturbed as he wondered what the future held for England. Henry's marriage to Anne had angered the papacy and driven a wedge between Rome and England but now that Anne was dead, if Jane Seymour had leanings towards Rome she could easily move the king. Would Henry turn back to Rome? Already the German Protestants had recoiled in horror at Henry's action and felt that this was a pledge of reconciliation offered to Rome by Henry.

Meanwhile the pope was transported with joy at Anne's death. 'I always thought, when I saw Henry endowed with so many virtues, that heaven would not forsake him,' he exclaimed. He even admitted that he, the infallible pope, had made a mistake when he made Fisher a cardinal and he told Henry's agent that, if the king made the least sign of reconciliation, he would send him a nuncio.[1] The stage was all set for Henry and England to be received back into the bosom of Rome. Campeggio, one time Bishop of Salisbury, cheered up and began to make plans for recovering his see.

A few weeks after Anne's death a book reached England called the *Unity of the Church*. It had been written some time previously but reached England only in June 1536, and its fierce denunciation of Henry made all hope of reconciliation with Rome impossible. The English people were urged

1. Papal ambassador.

to unite and rebel against Henry who was described as 'the
vilest of plunderers, a thief and a robber'. Its author,
Reginald Pole, later to become cardinal, was a distant relative
of Henry since his mother was daughter of George, Duke of
Clarence. Pole was a fanatical supporter of the papacy and
had written the book in defence of Henry's marriage to
Catherine. It was long delayed and it made him seem more
like a supporter of Anne. It was a masterpiece of sarcastic
and indignant invective and Pole had been advised not to
have it published. Naturally, Henry was furious when it was
brought to him. 'There are two churches: if you are at the
head of one, it is not the church of Christ; if you are, it is like
Satan, who is the prince of the world. . . . Neither Nero nor
Domitian, nor — I dare affirm — Luther himself, if he had
been King of England, would have wished to avenge himself
by putting to death such men as Fisher and Sir Thomas
More!' One hundred and ninety-two folio pages of a tirade
written in this style was hardly likely to draw Henry back to
Rome. If he had hesitated before, his mind was now firmly
made up.

On 9 June 1536 the first Convocation assembled since the
break with the papacy. Cranmer wisely decided that Latimer
was the ideal man to preach the opening sermon. It was a day
that called for boldness; the majority of those gathered were
still Catholics at heart and reluctant to accept the fact that
the break with Rome was permanent. No one could see more
clearly than Latimer the abuses that needed to be reformed
and he was unlikely to be timid in his preaching. Four years
previously he had stood there accused of heresy; before him
sat the men who had tried him. The very memories must have
added strength to his eloquence.

Latimer chose for his text the parable of the unjust
steward and bluntly told the prelates that they were equally
unjust and unfaithful. He asked what they had done for the
English people in the last seven years. Were the people better
taught? Had they preached more faithfully as ordered by the
king? He even dared to remind them that they would have
burnt him if they could because he supported the supremacy

of the king. The church was full of abuses which they and their forbears had invented: 'canonizations and expectations, pardons, stationaries and jubilaries'. Worst of all was 'old purgatory pick-purse' which emptied men's pockets and made the church rich.

'Is it so hard, is it so great a matter for you to see many abuses in the clergy, many in the laity? Abuses. . . in the images and pictures, and relics, and pilgrimages, extolled and encouraged by the clergy to the deception of the ignorant. . . . But,' concluded Latimer, 'be not deceived, God will come, God will come, He will not tarry long away. . . . Feed ye tenderly, with all diligence, the flock of Christ. Preach truly the Word of God. Love the light, walk in the light, and so be ye the children of light while ye are in this world. . . .'

Luther could not have spoken with more bluntness or plainness. Latimer had been trained as a youth to use the longbow, a weapon which takes all one's strength to draw back. Now he did the same in this sermon to Convocation and all his wit, learning and strength lay behind it. It was very far removed from the pleasant platitudes to which they were accustomed and, while he spoke in Latin, it was translated into English and his words soon spread throughout England. He had not gone into deep theology and basically he had attacked the lives of the clergy rather than their doctrine. The sermon was plainly understood by the ordinary people when it was relayed to them. The result was a cry for reformation from every corner of England. Latimer had been the voice of the people at Convocation.

The bishops' response was to draw up a list of heresies that they wanted dealt with, such as these: 'That priests should be allowed to marry;' 'That the laity should receive the communion in both kinds [that is, both the bread and the wine] ;' 'That images ought not to be reverenced.' Since Tyndale's New Testament and various Protestant tracts had been smuggled into England, many people had grasped these biblical doctrines and the prelates were becoming more alarmed. The bishops also complained about the circulation of heretical books, particularly the New Testament. Latimer's sermon had left them unmoved and they were determined to cling to their old ways and teaching.

But the very presence of Cromwell, the king's vicar-general who sat, not next to Cranmer but above them all, was a clear indication that the church was now *under* the Crown, and it should have warned them that Henry did not regard the royal supremacy as a mere empty title. Cromwell was well aware as Convocation progressed that the news of Latimer's sermon had reached the people, that throughout the country there was theological strife and debate and people were demanding the removal of the doctrinal errors which the bishops had defended. Henry was determined to obtain unity and peace and this was what Cromwell insisted Convocation must settle.

When he rose to speak, Cromwell reminded them of this: 'He (the king) desireth you, for Christ's sake, that all malice, obstinacy and carnal respect set apart, ye will friendly and lovingly dispute among yourselves of the controversies moved in the church, and that ye will conclude *all things by the Word of God*. . . . Neither will His Majesty suffer the Scripture to be wrested and defaced by any glosses, any papistical laws, or by any authority of doctors or councils; and much less will he admit any articles or doctrines not contained in the Scriptures, but approved only by continuance of time and old custom and by *unwritten verities*. . . .'

This was a momentous day for England. For the first time Convocation was ordered to use only the Word of God and tradition ('unwritten verities') was banned. It is significant that these words came, not from a clergyman, but a layman. The Reformation, while it depended on trained ministers to expound the Word, was a movement of the Spirit of God among all His people, and was equally dependent on the humblest Christians' reading and learning the Bible for themselves and teaching their children its truths.

The bishops were determined to maintain their medieval Roman Catholic doctrines. Stokesley endeavoured by twisting Scripture to prove that there were seven sacraments. He immediately forgot Cromwell's order and tried to strengthen his case by appealing to tradition. Cromwell had brought with him a Scottish theologian, Alesius, who had been driven from St Andrew's University for heresy and had taken refuge in Germany for a time, where he had become a friend of Melancthon. Henry received him courteously when he came to England and he was now living with Cranmer. As Alesius had been Reader of Divinity at Cambridge for a time, Cromwell introduced him to the prelates and asked him what he thought of the sacraments.

Alesius demonstrated clearly from Scripture that there were only two — baptism and the Lord's Supper. He was not only an ardent Reformer, but also perfectly familiar with the controversy that had raged across Europe. Like many Scottish theologians, he was admirably gifted as a speaker and enjoyed a good debate. Stokesley was furious and shouted out, 'All that is false!' Alesius was quite willing to expand his theme and show that Scripture and the writings of the old church fathers both supported his statements.

Fox, Bishop of Hereford, then rose to speak. He had just returned from Wittenberg where he had grasped the truth more firmly since he had met Luther and Melancthon. 'Think ye not that we can by any sophistical subtleties steal out of the world again the light which every man doth see. Christ hath so lightened the world at this time that the light of the gospel hath put to flight all misty darkness, and it will shortly have the higher hand of all clouds, though we resist in vain never so much. The lay people do know the Holy Scriptures better than many of us. And the Germans have made the text of the Bible so plain and easy by the Hebrew and the Greek tongue, that now many things may be better understood without any glosses at all than by all the commentaries of the doctors. And moreover they have so opened these controversies by their writings that women and children may wonder at the blindness and falsehood that hath been hitherto. . . .'

Alesius exclaimed, 'Yes, it is the Word of God that bringeth life; the Word of God is the very substance and body of the sacrament. It makes us certain and sure of the will of God to save our souls: the outward ceremony is but a token of

that lively inflammation which we receive through faith in
the Word and promise of the Lord.'

Stokesley could stand no more. He insisted that they were
deceived if they believed the Word of God was contained in
the Bible alone. Ten years later the Council of Trent, called by
the Counter-Reformation forces, put Stokesley's words in a
clearer form and stated, 'We must receive with similar respect
and equal piety the Holy Scriptures and tradition.'[2] This is
still taught by Rome.

A sharp debate ensued and when they broke up the
Roman Catholic prelates were angry at the part that Alesius
had played. Upon resumption of the debate it became clear
to Cromwell that for diplomatic reasons Alesius should withdraw. The result was that the bishops were unable to reach
any agreement.

'The lay people do know the Holy Scriptures better than
many of us,' Fox had said and the importance of this cannot
be overemphasized. Where people read the Bible free from
interpretation of the church leaders and the addition of
tradition, the Holy Spirit moved in their hearts. On 4
October 1535 Miles Coverdale's translation had appeared,
probably in Zurich, and about this time it reached England.

Unfortunately this translation was dedicated to Henry and
asked the divine blessing on him and his 'dearest just wife,
and most virtuous princess, Queen Anne'. As his 'dearest just
wife' had been beheaded it was impossible to distribute this
version. Some copies were changed with a pen to 'Queen
Jane' and others had the name scratched out. Later a new
title page was printed. It would appear that the king gave
verbal approval to this translation, unlike Tyndale's which he
hated, but he did nothing to have it officially recognized and
circulated. Despite this the Reformation was spreading as
pious ministers expounded the Word of God and taught the
people. Tyndale's translation was still being distributed
throughout the country. The English people were becoming
what J.R. Green described as 'the people of a book, and that

2. Council of Trent, 4th sitting, 8 April 1546.

book the Bible'. [3]

Henry was determined to find a solution to the rival parties at Convocation. If they could not find a creed satisfactory to all, he would draw one up himself. He had always had a keenness for theological debates and scholars are agreed that it was not flattery but fact when Henry was described as the author of the 'Ten Articles'. Five of the Articles dealt with doctrine and five with ceremonies and together they were the first doctrinal statement of the Church of England. Foxe, the martyrologist, describes them as meant for 'weaklings newly weaned from their mother's milk of Rome'. They were neither Roman enough to satisfy Stokesley nor biblical enough to please the more advanced Reformers.

The Bible, the Apostles', Nicene and Athanasian creeds and the decisions of the first four ecumenical councils were regarded as the standard of orthodoxy. Baptism was considered essential for salvation as was the sacrament of penance. The real corporeal presence of Christ's body and blood under the form of bread and wine in the Eucharist (Holy Communion) was taught. Faith as well as charity was needed for salvation, images and saint worship were still approved of and so was prayer to saints but, the new creed added, grace, remission of sin and salvation can only be obtained from God through Christ's mediation. Rites and ceremonies were to be retained and the doctrine of purgatory was reaffirmed, but the teaching that the pope's pardons or masses offered for the dead could help them was to be abolished utterly. As Professor T. M. Lindsay points out, 'While the Real Presence is maintained, nothing is said about transubstantiation.' [4] Despite the statements that make one feel that it was Roman Catholic, without the pope, it was a step in the right direction. The Articles did not teach that there were seven sacraments, but Rome still maintains that there are.

Most Englishmen accepted the Articles as representing

3. J. R. Green, *Short History of the English People*, 1892 edition.
4. T. M. Lindsay, *History of the Reformation* vol. ii, p. 334.

their beliefs and Latimer signed with the rest. It is worth noting that he appears to have been consulted on the subject of purgatory, although Henry chose not to accept his opinion. A letter is preserved containing Latimer's arguments against purgatory and Henry's criticisms of his views are written in the margin. Latimer rested his arguments on Scripture and on the teachings of the greatest church fathers. He admitted that some of the latter appeared to sanction purgatory but he claimed the right to differ from them and protested against giving to them the authority which belonged to Scripture alone. Henry's replies are feeble, rather like a schoolboy's quibble with his master.[5] This letter shows that Latimer was growing in biblical knowledge, albeit slowly.

Convocation gave its approval to the Ten Articles and the parish priests were ordered to teach them to the people. As one writer says, 'They were meant to wean the people, if gradually, from the gross superstition which disgraced the popular medieval religion.' Under the Injunctions issued by Cromwell, Latimer was anxious to return to his diocese, when Convocation rose on 20 July, to ensure that his priests taught the people as the king had commanded. He had some hard work ahead as many idle monks, thrown loose upon society, had begun to preach against the Reformers and Latimer had to take severe steps to curb their activity in the summer and autumn of 1536.

The Injunctions strengthened his hand in reforming his diocese since they discouraged people from pilgrimages. It pleased God better, they were told, if they worked hard and provided for their families, and it was more beneficial for their souls if they helped the poor rather than giving money to images. This was what Latimer had wanted for years — practical reformation that everyone could understand.

This pastoral work was rudely interrupted in October when a small insurrection led by a shoemaker called Melton, or Captain Cobbler, broke out in Lincolnshire. The insurgents complained at the dissolution of the monasteries and the

5. Latimer, *Remains*, p. 245.

changes made in religion. This was soon dealt with but almost immediately a more formidable revolt broke out in Yorkshire. 'The Pilgrimage of Grace', as it was called, made similar demands on the king — a return to the old ways and old doctrines, with the re-establishment of the pope. Many dispossessed priests led this and only one person from the nobility, the Earl of Northumberland, remained faithful to the king. The others, with the Archbishop of York, acted as leaders and people flocked to join the rebels. It was a concerted attack by the Catholic powers — 30,000 rebels were on the march and Henry was unable to raise one third of this number in troops. It looked as if the House of Tudor must fall to the Catholic forces.

Latimer was summoned to London to preach against the rebels and encourage loyal subjects. On 5 November 1536 he preached at Paul's Cross using the text: 'Put on the whole armour of God.' It is not considered one of his best sermons as he had to choose his words carefully, but it encouraged the people of London. The insurgents were delayed by a sudden flood of the river Don, but the Duke of Norfolk used great wisdom when he eventually met the rebels and, in consequence of threats and promises, they gradually dispersed. By January 1537 tranquillity was restored but many of the leaders went to the gallows or the block. A king who beheaded his queen had no mercy for rebels.

But a great blow was about to be struck against the Reformers. Tyndale, who had given England the New Testament, and had been confined in a dungeon since May 1535, was tried in August 1536 by an ecclesiastical court, condemned and unfrocked. On 6 October 1536 he was taken from the castle at Vilvorde to be strangled and burned. Even at the stake he had but one thought and prayed, 'Lord, open the King of England's eyes!' Almost immediately he was put to death. One hears echoes of Stephen's words in this. 'William Tyndale,' Foxe records, 'who, for his notable pains and travail, may well be called the Apostle of England in this our later age.'

Latimer suffered grave misgivings when he heard of

Tyndale's death. His passing boded ill for the Reformation cause.

13. The 'Bloody Statute'

June 1537 – July 1539

The enemies of the Reformation were looking for fresh prey. During the rebellion in the North there were clergy in Latimer's diocese, especially in Bristol, who were fiercely opposed to the Reformation. While they did not take up arms, they denounced Latimer as the chief patron and fountain of the heresy in his diocese. 'The Bishop of Worcester is a heretic, and it is a pity he has not been burned.' said one. 'I trust to bring a faggot,' said another priest, 'and to see the Bishop of Worcester burned, and it is a pity that he was ever born.'[1] With clergy acting in this insubordinate manner, Latimer's life was far from easy. It was soon found that the Ten Articles were too ambiguous and cunning priests interpreted them as they pleased. Instead of promoting unity they brought about division.

Neither Parliament nor Convocation met in 1537, but in April Latimer was summoned to a commission of divines to prepare better articles of religion. Alas, there was no Alesius this time, neither was Cromwell present, and the debates dragged on interminably. Latimer appears to have taken little part in these as he had not yet studied in detail the great theological differences between Rome and the Reformers. His life had been a busy one and he had always been a man for the practical side of Christianity, having not yet realized that a Christian must have firm doctrinal foundations for his faith.

Suddenly he was ordered to go to the Tower and speak to the leaders of the 'Pilgrimage of Grace' who were awaiting execution. This pastoral ministry was work close to Latimer's

1. *Cromwell's papers*, State Paper Office.

heart. He visited a number of the prisoners and spoke with them for a long time but we have no record of any results. Soon afterwards they were executed.

In July a book appeared which expounded the Apostles' Creed, the seven sacraments, the Ten Commandments, the Lord's Prayer and the *Ave Maria*. This catechism was prepared by a committee of divines and was expected to have the royal sanction. For some reason it did not receive this and, when published, came to be known as the *Bishops' Book*. It constituted a backward step since it emphasized that there were seven sacraments, while the Ten Articles declared that there were only three. It conceded more to Rome than to the Reformers but we must remember that in 1537 even Cranmer and Latimer believed as firmly in transubstantiation as did Rome. Their growth was slow compared to that of the Continental Reformers and it was some time before they abandoned this and other Roman Catholic doctrines.

It had been a disappointing year for Latimer and he was anxious to return to Worcester and get away from the debates. But before he left London his cup of joy overflowed. Richard Grafton, a printer, had an audience with Cranmer in August to show him a 'new translation of the Bible in new print', and asked that he would obtain the king's consent to have it sold and read freely. Cranmer read the new translation and liked it. He sent it to Cromwell and besought him to persuade Henry to give his approval. The amazing thing is that Henry did so, and speedily, too! He had run his eyes over the pages — Tyndale's name was not there and the dedication to the king was well written, so he authorized the sale and reading of this Bible. It had been prepared by John Rogers, a friend of Tyndale; he had used Tyndale's translation of the Old Testament books that he had completed, filling in the blanks in the Old Testament from Coverdale's version, and published it — together with Tyndale's New Testament translation — under the name of Thomas Matthew. Most of this Bible was therefore Tyndale's own fine scholarly work which Henry had always hated! Latimer saw this Bible and was full of gratitude. 'Lord, open the King of England's eyes,'

Tyndale had prayed. God had answered the martyr's prayer.

* * * * * * *

In October a cry of joy went up from Hampton Court and was echoed throughout England. Jane Seymour had given birth to a boy, Edward, on 12 October 1537. At last Henry had the male heir for whom he longed. He had reigned twenty-eight years, Elizabeth and Mary had been declared illegitimate and Henry's health was declining. Without an heir civil war would probably have taken place when Henry died and the Roman party believed that God had denied him a male heir because of his wickedness in breaking with Rome. Now all was changed. The people looked forward to an undisputed succession and stable government. Unfortunately Jane lived only twelve days after Edward's birth and Henry was grief-stricken.

Latimer, although far from well, was summoned to preach in London on 13 November, the day after the queen's funeral. He also had business to transact with Cromwell. In his letters to Cromwell Latimer refers to 'a good nurse, good Mistress Statham, which seeing what case I was in, hath fetched me home to her own house, and doth pamper me up with all diligence. . .'. Mistress Statham, a married woman, was an admiring follower of Latimer and his teaching. Her kindness to him was not forgotten when Mary ascended the throne. The Roman Catholic party noted all who helped the Reformers and later took their revenge.

1538 was one of the busiest years in Latimer's episcopate, and certainly it marked great progress for the Reformation. It could be said that this was the year in which the Reformation reached its highest point during Henry's reign. Progress could have been even greater had the king not been so stubborn regarding changes. The German Protestants sought unity with England and Cranmer was keen to see this take place. But after long talks Henry still refused to allow the laity to have the cup at communion. He also insisted on private masses and the celibacy of the clergy. On these rocks the proposed alliance foundered.

Latimer spent Christmas at Worcester with his old friend Prior Barnes, who had returned to England. In February 1538 he was summoned to take part in an unusual service in London. Latimer had always been a keen preacher but when he knew the purpose of this service he could have jumped for joy. For years he had denounced pilgrimages to relics and images of Mary or some saint. Now Cranmer and Cromwell had resolved to bring the most infamous images into discredit and show them up before the public as pieces of trickery. Every county had its local deity, reputed to have miraculous powers. By means of wires and concealed machinery the priests caused the images to wink, nod and even shed tears. People believed in these seemingly marvellous powers and, after reverencing the images and leaving an offering, they believed that they went away healed, in much the same way as pilgrims do at Lourdes today.

The Rood (crucifix) of Bexley, in Kent, stood in high repute in the South of England. It is best described in a verse of the time:

> He was made to juggle,
> His eyes would goggle,
>   He would bend his brows and frown
> With his head he would nod
> Like a proper young god,
>   His chafts [jaws] would go up and down.

One of Cromwell's visitors first detected this fraud and took the image into Maidstone on market day to show the people how they had been deceived. It was decided to make a more public exhibition of this image, so it was brought to London. Hilsey, now Bishop of Rochester, preached the sermon and 'explained all the trickery and imposture in the presence of the people. . . after all its tricks had been exposed to the people, it was broken into small pieces. . . . After this, Bishop Latimer, in the western part of St Paul's, carried a small image in his hand, which he threw out of the church.' [2]

2. *Zurich Letters*, p. 606.

This was the beginning of a great purge in England, at least in those dioceses where the bishops supported the Reformation. Latimer spent a large part of 1538 in examining relics, and showing simple people how they had been deceived, and also in preaching against idolatry. With poor health and these extra duties, Latimer was glad that the new law permitted the appointment of assistant or suffragan bishops for the large dioceses. Henry Holbeach, Prior of Worcester, was appointed in March to assist him.

In a letter to Cromwell dated 13 June, Latimer refers to 'Our great Sibyl. . . she hath been the devil's instrument to bring many, I fear, to eternal fire. . .'. 'Our great Sibyl' was a famous statue of the Virgin which stood in Worcester Cathedral, held to be most sacred and visited by scores of pilgrims. On Cromwell's orders it was stripped of the gaudy trappings in which ignorant people arrayed it and underneath they found only the statue of some unknown bishop! 'Sibyl' was taken to Chelsea in company with 'her old sister of Walsingham' (another image) and publicly burned while the people jeered. They were slowly beginning to see how they and their forefathers had been deceived.

One more example will suffice to show how much work Latimer had to do and how much deception and superstition was inflicted on the English people. In September 1538 he went with others to the monastery of Hales, in Gloucestershire to investigate the 'Blood of Hales', another famous relic venerated all over the West of England. This had vexed Latimer for years; when he was the poor parson of West Kington it had grieved him to see his parishioners going to worship and leave offerings before this relic.

The monks pretended that they had some of Christ's blood in a bottle and thousands of penitents came to see it. When a rich man confessed to the priest and laid his gift on the altar, he was taken to the chapel where this precious vessel stood in a case. The penitent looked at it but saw nothing. 'Your sin is not yet forgiven,' the priest would say. More money was laid on the altar and, when the monks were satisfied, the penitent saw the supposed blood of Christ gleaming from the glass.

This imposture was found by the Commissioners to be made of 'a crystal very thick on one side and very transparent on the other', filled with melted honey coloured with saffron. 'When a rich man appears,' explained the monk, 'we turn the vessel on the thick side; that, you know, opens his heart and his purse.' This wicked fraud was denounced by Hilsey when he preached at Paul's Cross and people were invited to examine it and see how they had been duped.

Henry, now a widower, had been looking for another suitable princess to take Jane's place. Several young women on the Continent were suggested and approached, but every time the terms were too high. Henry must first be reconciled to Rome.

In September 1538 the king made a decision that damned him for ever in the eyes of the Catholics and caused the pope to excommunicate him in December. Henry decided that he *would* make the Bible available to all his subjects. For once he kept his word. On 5 September 1538 a second series of Injunctions were issued to the clergy by Cromwell: 'Item, that you shall provide on this side the feast of Easter next coming, one book of the whole Bible of the largest volume, in English, and the same set up in some convenient place within the said church that you have cure of, whereas your parishioners may most commodiously resort to the same, and read it. . . .' [3] No one was to be dissuaded from reading this Bible, on the contrary, all were to be encouraged to read it. This was a momentous day for England and for the Reformation. The Word of God which brings light and life was to be available to all Englishmen. The printing of this Bible is a story in itself; suffice it to say here that it was printed and placed in the churches the following April.

It was just in time. In September 1538 Latimer's old enemy Gardiner, the Bishop of Winchester, returned to England. He was the man for whom the Catholics had been looking. He had been away three years and the Catholics had been unable to meet the determination of Cromwell, Cranmer

3. H. Bettensen, *Documents of the Christian Church*, p. 325.

and Latimer. Now they had their man and he threw his learning, shrewdness and cunning into the fight to prevent Henry
from moving any further towards the Reformed position. He
was never a favourite with Henry, who distrusted him, but he
often gained the king's ear and the Catholics rallied round
him. Gardiner could see that there was no hope of reunion
with Rome but he fought tooth and nail to bring Henry and
England back to Catholicism minus the pope.

He wasted no time. There were a number of Continental
Christians in England who were more advanced in their theology than Latimer or Cranmer, mainly because they based all
their doctrine on the Bible and disregarded tradition. Some
of these were called Anabaptists since they believed only in
believers' baptism; they also believed that church and state
should be completely separate, denied transubstantiation and
held views on the communion which were very similar to
those held by the Swiss Reformers.

To avoid confusion, it must be made clear that the Anabaptists were not the first English Baptists. The latter broke
away from the Puritans about 1606 as they felt that the Puritans still clung to some of the non-biblical teachings of the
Anglican church — the union of church and state, government by diocesan bishops and the acceptance of every baptized person as a 'Christian'. But most of all they disagreed
with the Puritans concerning the baptism of infants. The
first English Baptists seceded from the Puritans and founded
churches formed of those who had been baptized (by immer-
sion) after they had confessed their faith in Christ.[4] On the
other hand, Anabaptists (re-baptizers) came from the Continent. The name was given to small groups of Christians that
sprung up and formed small churches composed only of
those who had confessed their faith in Christ when they were
baptized. But Anabaptists had roots that can be traced back
several centuries before the Reformation.[5] They rejected the
inclusive idea of the Roman church and of the Lutheran and

---

4. A. C. Underwood, *A History of the English Baptists*, pp. 15-40.
5. T. M. Lindsay, *A History of the Reformation*, vol. ii, pp. 235ff.

Calvinist churches where infants were baptized and then regarded as members of the church. They baptized only those who had a definite experience of Christ's saving power and who asked to be baptized after they were converted. A basic tenet of the Anabaptists was their insistence on each person's direct accountability to God. They recognized no other mediator than Jesus Christ, so they opposed clericalism and priests. This led them to insist on the right of the individual to interpret Scripture for himself.

Mainly because they rejected the Roman church and also insisted on the separation of church and state, they were violently persecuted in Holland, Germany, Switzerland — in fact wherever they appeared. Because they lost most of their educated leaders through the brutality of the authorities, many of those who survived were humble artificers with no training in theology. One result of this was that some of them brought forward heretical teachings that had been condemned centuries before. For example, one of their leaders, Melchior Hoffman, laid so much emphasis on our Lord's deity that he virtually denied His humanity. Many of his followers did the same and speculated on the Incarnation of Christ, but many of them were orthodox on all essential doctrines.

On 1 October 1538 a number of these foreign Anabaptists were tried by a commission which included Cranmer, Barnes, Crome and certain others, but not Latimer. Two were made to bear faggots to Paul's Cross and two were burned at the stake. Tolerance was still a word unknown among the Reformers, but it is highly probable that Gardiner's hand was behind these events.

Rumours had been circulating that Henry had changed his beliefs and had adopted the biblical teaching of the Swiss Reformers. Gardiner saw his opportunity and suggested to the king that he should openly show his orthodoxy by dealing ruthlessly with any who denied the real corporeal presence of Christ in the sacrament of the mass. Henry soon found a victim, Lambert, one of Bilney's converts. He was an able and zealous Reformer but he was caught denying the real presence and was arrested and taken to Lambeth

for trial. He was told that he must either recant or be condemned as a heretic, since the Articles maintained this
doctrine. However reluctant Cranmer might have been to
condemn Lambert, he had little choice as Henry had decided
to come and sit as a theological judge.

A Royal Commission was appointed to try Lambert and
Henry was chairman. 'Is the sacrament of the altar the body
of Christ or not?' Henry asked. 'After a certain manner, it is
the body of Christ, as St Augustine has said,' Lambert
replied. 'Answer me not out of St Augustine,' the king
snapped, 'Tell me plainly, is it the body of Christ or not?'
Lambert denied that it was and Cranmer tried to persuade
him of his error. Then Gardiner, Tunstall and Stokesley
attacked him fiercely. He was found guilty and burned at
Smithfield on 20 November 1538. There is no record of
Latimer taking any part in this trial but we wonder what
effect the trial and debate had on his views and how it helped
him to move towards the biblical teaching of the Lord's
Supper.

Gardiner was elated over this success. Not only had he
prevented Henry from moving towards the biblical doctrine,
but he had frustrated any hope of alliance with the
Continental Reformers. Moreover he had succeeded in
making Cromwell and Cranmer assist him in condemning a
man they valued and esteemed.

Despite Gardiner's elation, this trial and debate had not
been in vain. Cranmer, who had been unconvinced by the
writings and arguments of the Continental Reformers, had
been shaken by Lambert's arguments and his consistency
when he knew that he faced a terrible death. So Lambert's
martyrdom caused Cranmer and the other Reformers to look
more closely at Scripture and this eventually led them to
abandon the central doctrine of the Roman church, the
sacrifice of the mass.

But this was only one side of the coin. Henry followed his
condemnation of Lambert by laying down narrow lines of
demarcation for both Reformers and Catholics. These were
strictly enforced; all had to bend the knee and submit to the

royal decree. No one, unless learned in divinity, was to 'dispute or argue upon the sacrament of the altar', if he did he would die. Henry struck out in both directions. People had to observe the customary ceremonies, creeping to the cross on Good Friday, carrying candles on the Feast of Purification and similar Roman rites. A number of priests had married; they were to lose their livings and become lay persons. On the other hand Thomas-à-Becket was denounced as a rebel and not a saint, and his image and name were removed from churches and service books. Gardiner hoped the king would go further and revive Roman ceremonies and some prelates prepared a book of ceremonies. The Reformers felt that their sky was becoming dark indeed.

But when 1539 began Henry, in his customary stop-start fashion, was again holding out the olive branch to the German Protestants simply because he was interested in a German princess, Anne of Cleves, who might become his wife. He received a poor welcome from the Germans. Melancthon wrote to warn him that the use of Roman ceremonies was more likely to restore reverence for the pope, who had introduced them, than to help the English people. Henry should allow liberty of opinion to his people in non-essentials.

The king had always wanted unity in the English church and in May he tried, by means of a committee, to draw up new articles which would heal the divisions. As nine commissioners were named, of whom five were rigid Catholics, it was doomed to failure. Neither side would give way and Henry's patience was soon exhausted. Politics, too, played their part in making Henry step into the theological field again. Rome had entered into an alliance with the emperor and the King of France. If the pope put pressure on France and the Low Countries, all trade to England might cease unless Henry returned to the church. This worried him and he decided to come down firmly on the Catholic side.

Six Articles were drawn up and the Duke of Norfolk introduced them to the House of Lords. 'I have never read the holy Scriptures and I never will read them,' he declared. 'All that I want is that everything should be as it was of old.' This shows Norfolk's position, he was Catholic to the core. It shows, too, the nature of the Six Articles, which were both reactionary and Catholic. These Articles insisted on: 1. The real presence of Christ in the sacrament; 2. Denial of the cup to the laity; 3. Celibacy of the clergy; 4. The obligation of monastic vows; 5. The benefit of private masses, and 6. Auricular confession.

These Articles put England back years and they were well named 'the Whip with Six Strings' and 'the Bloody Statute' by the Reformers. All the Reformers opposed them vehemently, even though Henry himself was present during much of the debate. Cranmer, Latimer and Shaxton advocated the views on communion which they were beginning to believe, while Gardiner, Tunstall and Stokesley maintained the Roman teaching. After all the debates the bill was passed by the Lords and, while the Commons opposed it to some extent, they also passed it. On 28 June 1539 it received the royal assent and became law. Neither Cranmer nor Latimer signed or consented to these Articles.

While Parliament was assembled, Henry also lashed out at the Catholics by getting Parliament to agree that the Crown should take all the remaining monasteries. His principal motive was greed as, if valued today, they would be worth many million pounds.

Latimer was grief-stricken by these new Articles. He had nothing to fear concerning the first Article, since he still leaned towards the Roman teaching; he was unmarried so he did not need to worry about the harshness to married priests, but as a bishop he would have to sit and judge others whom he respected and loved. He was in a cleft stick unless he made a firm decision. His health was deteriorating and he had always preferred to preach rather than to rule in the church. There is some dispute among historians as to whether Latimer was misinformed and told that Henry wanted his resignation, but the facts that emerge are that the bill became law on 28 June and on 1 July Latimer resigned his bishopric. Some have praised him for this action, others have accused him of weakness. Foxe says that as he left off his episcopal robes he gave a skip on the floor for joy. 'Now I am rid of a heavy burden,' he said.

Latimer's resignation angered Henry. He disliked bishops who refused to obey his orders, and Latimer was ordered to be kept in ward in the house of the Bishop of Chichester in London. He had become a prisoner.

14. *Fugitive bishop*

1539 — 1547

While Henry was angry with Latimer, he was fearful lest Cranmer should also resign, so he sent for the archbishop and received him graciously. Henry assured Cranmer that he still held him in high esteem and admired the learning that he showed in the debates. If Cranmer resigned Henry would have to choose another primate and that would be a difficult task. Gardiner would jump at the opportunity but, as we have seen, Henry distrusted him. In any case, to appoint a new archbishop without the pope would be far from easy, despite Henry's new role. So, while the king disagreed with Cranmer, he kept him as primate.

With bishops it was different; hence Latimer's imprisonment. He was not kept in strict confinement but, while he could not go out, his friends were allowed to visit him. A number of them were convinced that he should not have resigned and tried to persuade him to submit to the king and obtain his liberty — perhaps even regain his bishopric. Latimer refused to be swayed since he had counted the cost and made his decision. He remained a prisoner until the spring of 1540 when Sampson, Bishop of Chichester, was himself sent to the Tower, after which event Latimer appears to have been allowed a greater measure of freedom. His heart must have been gladdened by the fact that, despite attempts by the Roman party to have the Bible banned, the king had declared that it must continue to be freely available to all 'for their own instruction and edification' and that no one was to be hindered in any way.

The Six Articles horrified the Continental Reformers, who declared them barbarous. Melancthon wrote to Henry, exhorting him to reconsider his action and comparing the

Articles with the teaching of Rome. He also spoke bluntly to Henry about the imprisonment of such men as Latimer and Shaxton, the very 'lanthorns of light' to the Church of England. Another act was passed which took heretics from the jurisdiction of the bishops and placed them under the power of the secular courts — the only occurrence that could have pleased the Continental Reformers. This resulted in about five hundred people being set at liberty. The Continental Reformers soon had an opportunity to hear firsthand what had taken place in England, since most of the more ardent Reformers decided that they could no longer live in England under such laws. They had about two weeks before the Six Articles became law, and during that time many left the country for Germany or Switzerland. They found refuge in Zurich, Basle and Strasbourg and their contact with the other Reformers was to have a great effect on the English Reformation as they learned much from their Continental brethren. On their eventual return to England they brought with them new biblical teaching on many matters.

Cromwell, always active in church and state, at last succeeded in finding a suitable princess for Henry. The king had been a widower for nearly two years and, after seeing an exquisite miniature of Anne of Cleves, painted by Holbein, he decided that he would marry her. Anne, daughter of the Duke of Cleves and sister-in-law of the Elector of Saxony, Luther's protector, possessed the necessary religious and political qualifications demanded by Henry. Cromwell made all requisite arrangements; Anne consented and came to England at the end of 1539.

Henry was horrified when he saw her. Anne had coarse features, a brown complexion, she was corpulent and her manners, too, lacked refinement. The king felt only revulsion for her. Cromwell and the courtiers had flattered her, as had Holbein's painting. Henry felt duty-bound to go through with the marriage ceremony on 6 January 1540 but it was more like a funeral service as the king was so mournful and downcast. His sole comfort was that he could now be allied with the Protestant princes on the Continent, if he could persuade them to modify their doctrine.

For a short time this marriage gave the Reformers greater freedom than they had previously enjoyed, since Henry wished to appear as generous to the Protestants as were his Continental counterparts. In fact the 'Bloody Statute' was virtually suspended and Latimer may well have regretted the resignation of his see. However, this state of affairs did not last for long. Henry kept up an outward display of courtesy towards Anne while he decided on his next move. By April 1540 it was apparent to all that she dissatisfied him and the following month he openly deserted her. Henry remembered Cromwell's part in arranging the marriage and it was to prove another nail in his coffin.

Cranmer and the Reformers were greatly disappointed as they believed Anne to be a Christian and hoped that with her influence the gospel might be spread more widely. Latimer's old friend Barnes had also taken part in the negotiations for Anne's betrothal, so Henry accorded him part of the blame. Barnes never lost the ability to say the wrong thing at the wrong time. He was rash in his preaching and enjoyed extra liberty that spring. Gardiner preached at Paul's Cross in February and attacked the Reformed doctrines. Three weeks later Barnes preached in the same pulpit and defended these doctrines. He also made sarcastic remarks about Gardiner while he and the Lord Mayor of London sat and listened. Gardiner went straight to Henry to complain and Barnes was committed to the Tower to await the king's pleasure.

A few days later a more distinguished victim arrived at the Tower. On 10 June Cromwell was accused of high treason, arrested and sent to the Tower. There has been much debate as to Cromwell's offence but it is generally believed that it was, first, promoting Henry's marriage to Anne and, second, opposing Henry's contemplated divorce. For, in true Henrician fashion, the king had already been captivated by another young woman, Catherine Howard, niece of the Duke of Norfolk.

Cromwell had few friends; the Lords regarded him as an upstart, 'the blacksmith's son', and the bills he had passed through the Commons had gained him no friends. There is in fact a strong parallel between the fall of Wolsey and that of Cromwell. Both served the king well but were disposed of when they opposed one of his proposed marriages. Cranmer appears to be the only person who sought to defend Cromwell, whom he regarded not only as a personal friend, but also as a friend of the Reformation, as well as the most gifted servant of the king. Cranmer knew it was foolish to defend Cromwell but he wrote to Henry and reminded him of all that Cromwell had done for him. It is good to see the courage that Cranmer displayed at this time as he was always a weak man.

All was in vain. A bill of attainder was passed which denounced Cromwell as a 'false and corrupt traitor'. No evidence of any weight was brought against him and he was not even tried since, ironically, under an infamous law which Cromwell himself had passed, those accused of treason could be condemned without trial. On 28 July 1540 Cromwell perished on the scaffold, quietly committing his soul to God. He did much for England and laboured to obtain for her a reformed church and a free Bible.

Two days after Cromwell's death London saw a strange sight. Three hurdles were dragged through the streets to Smithfield. On these hurdles, side by side with three ardent Catholics, lay Barnes, Jerome and Garret. Henry had decided that the three Reformers must die, although he maintained that he supported neither Roman nor Reformed parties. How could he do this if, after executing Cromwell, he then put three Reformers to death? He had a brainwave; he would take three Catholics and put them to death with the Reformers, thereby showing the world his impartiality. Hence the three hurdles — a Protestant and a Catholic lay together on each.

At Smithfield they were unbound and, as they had been denied a trial, Barnes asked the sheriff if he might speak. He then addressed the people. He confessed his orthodoxy and denied any heresy. He also emphasized that he trusted only in Christ's finished work for his salvation. 'I do not doubt but through Him to inherit the kingdom of heaven,'[1] Barnes exclaimed. The three Reformers were then bound to one stake and died with patience and constancy. The three Catholics were hanged.

Latimer, in the Bishop of Chichester's house, heard with great sadness of Barnes's death. Letters appear to have passed between them because, despite Barnes's impetuousity, Latimer continued to love and respect him as a true servant of Christ. These letters put Latimer in considerable danger since any friend of a condemned heretic could be regarded as a heretic himself. He knew his own danger and told King Edward years later in a sermon, 'I looked every day to be called to execution.' Some courtier, probably Cranmer, appears to have made intercession to the king on Latimer's behalf and the danger passed. It is unclear what happened to him after this. Some think that he was given complete liberty, and he may have lived with Cranmer for a time, or with his old 'nurse' Mrs Statham. One fact, however, is clear: in July 1540 a general pardon was issued to all offenders, apart from the Anabaptists and Sacramentaries, and Latimer would then have been set at liberty, if not before. One clause in this pardon forbad him to preach or come within six miles of Oxford or Cambridge, the City of London or his old diocese. Like the great Puritan preachers a century later, Latimer was condemned to silence for the rest of Henry's reign.

While we have no definite knowledge of his life from July 1540 to May 1546, it would appear from the few fragments of records that we possess that he spent his time quietly visiting the houses of some of his hospitable country friends. They were glad to have under their roof a preacher whose words had once shaken the nation. Latimer for his part, while regretting his enforced silence, may well have welcomed the opportunity to spend more time studying the Bible and the works of the Continental Reformers. His life had been so busy that he had had little time for study but now he could read and meditate on the great doctrines of Scripture and so establish

1. Foxe, *Acts and Monuments* vol. v, p. 435.

a firmer foundation for his faith. Like a field which is left fallow for a time, he benefited from this period of relative inactivity. As he subjected his mind to the teachings of Scripture, the Roman doctrines gradually disappeared. When he again came into the public eye after Edward ascended the throne, Latimer's preaching contained a depth which was the result of this enforced retirement.

Although Henry had deserted Anne, he wished it to appear that he had left her for reasons of conscience. He set the necessary wheels in motion among his ministers in July and the matter was brought before Convocation. Gardiner was anxious to see a Roman Catholic queen on the throne and the clergy knew that apart from the 'king's conscience', Henry had eyes for Catherine Howard. After bringing forward many witnesses, Convocation decided that Henry had never given his 'inward consent' to the marriage and the 'sacrament of matrimony' was therefore utterly null and void. Cranmer, having just seen Cromwell arrested, did not dare to oppose the others. Anne was given a pension and the palace at Richmond, to which she retired.

Henry did not escape the sarcasm of the other princes of Europe about his treatment of Anne. 'It appears,' said Francis I of France, 'that over there they are pleased to do with women as with their geldings — bring a number of them together and make them trot, and then take the one which goes easiest.'

It is believed that Henry had first seen his latest 'gelding', Catherine Howard, at a banquet given by Gardiner to celebrate his marriage with Anne of Cleves. Gardiner had noted the impression she had made on the king and he and the Catholic party sought to promote Catherine's influence on the king. They had little need to encourage Henry since, once he set eyes on a woman he liked, he became an impetuous and impassioned lover. Citizens of London were more than scandalized to see Henry cross over the Thames by day as well as by night to see his new love. No sooner was the marriage with Anne annulled than he proceeded to his fifth betrothal. On 8 August 1540 he married Catherine and she was presented at court the same day.

Catherine was hailed with delight by the Catholic party. Now, after three Protestant queens, they had a Catholic one and hoped to see the church recover her power. In honour of Catherine, Henry became once more a devout Catholic and many ceremonies stopped by Cromwell and Cranmer were re-established — the consecration of bread and water, the embers with which the priests marked the foreheads of the faithful and other Roman rites. Under the influence of Gardiner and Catherine, England was swinging back towards Rome. The Reformers seemed to be threatened with the full violence of the 'Bloody Statute'.

Providentially Gardiner was sent abroad as a diplomat and did not return until October 1541. Nevertheless many people were imprisoned for neglecting the old ceremonies of the church, for reading the Bible aloud — despite the king's command that people should be encouraged to read it — and similar offences. Bonner, the new Bishop of London, was behind this. He had served under Cromwell and, now that he had become bishop, he sought to show that he did not support the doctrine that Cromwell had propagated. His zeal proved to be his undoing, since there were too many prisoners and even Henry did not consider burning five hundred people at once! Bonner had neglected certain legal formalities and eventually only a few were made to bear faggots or to go to the stake.

Henry felt that his latest marriage was like a glorious sixteen-month honeymoon and told his courtiers that he had never known such happiness. Catherine had the vivacity of Anne Boleyn and a lively temperament. To a man who was rapidly becoming a confirmed invalid she gave much pleasure. He was rudely awakened from this dream when Cranmer wrote to him and revealed that evidence had been laid before him of the queen's misconduct before marriage, and probably after it as well. The Privy Council had heard of this and had decided that Cranmer must break the news to the king. Henry was thunderstruck and burst into tears. The unhappy queen was committed to the Tower and a Parliament was called to decide her guilt. Parliament met on 16 January 1542 and the evidence was so overwhelming that Catherine was speedily declared guilty. The wretched queen, who was still comparatively young, was ordered to be beheaded and Henry once more became a widower.

The king's feelings towards the Catholic party then underwent a rapid change. Just as Catherine had influenced him to become a devout Catholic, so now he swung away and viewed them with suspicion. The diplomacy and caution displayed by Cranmer in the matter of Catherine increased the king's trust and liking for him.

Despite the suspicion with which Henry had come to view the Catholics, when Convocation assembled Gardiner came out with a new idea. He read to the clergy a list of words in the Bible which he proposed should be left in Latin on account of 'the majesty of the matter contained in them'. This was but the first step with Gardiner, who hoped eventually to have the Bible completely suppressed. He thought that if he could make the version in use sufficiently obscure, people would not understand what they read so would discontinue reading it. Gardiner wanted to introduce about one hundred Latin words such as *ecclesia, penitentia, pontifex, confessio* and *hostia*. It was not merely to obscure the English version that these were suggested, but because certain words were linked with Roman Catholic dogma and if he could retain the words he might retain the dogma too. All was to no avail, however, as Cranmer referred the matter to the king, who withdrew the power to revise the Bible from the bishops and promised to send the translation to the universities.

In 1543 it looked as if Gardiner would be successful, since an act was passed ordering all translations by Tyndale to be destroyed, and greatly limiting the freedom that people had previously enjoyed. This was a retrograde step but there proved to be so many loopholes in the act that people were able to evade the penalties of the law. It showed England, however, the anxiety of the Roman party to oppose the Reformation and suppress the Bible.

Although now in his early fifties, Henry — despite five marriages which had all ended tragically — was again looking for a wife. After the immorality of Catherine Howard a law had been passed which struck fear into the hearts of girls throughout England. The king was unable to find a young woman prepared to risk marriage with him so he decided to marry a widow. Catherine Parr, a lady of about thirty, had been twice widowed but she was beautiful and accomplished. She was, above all things, a woman of great piety who loved the gospel that the Reformers preached. She did, however, lack prudence at times and her zeal for the gospel made her forget what a temperamental man she was about to wed. Henry married her on 12 July 1543 but his bodily ailments and generally declining state meant that the queen had to be his nurse much of the time.

Henry found Catherine to be a kind and virtuous woman who faithfully discharged her duties as his wife. She also sought to influence him to be more lenient towards the Reformers. She sometimes failed and she certainly risked her own life many times. Still, it would appear that the queen's influence lessened the ferocity of some of the acts against the Reformers and brightened their prospects. Cranmer was delighted and admired Catherine, but she filled Gardiner with alarm and he became even more zealous to maintain the Catholic doctrines.

However, in 1544 Gardiner's nephew was accused of treason and executed as a traitor, and this cast a shadow over the zealous Catholic, who was suspected of being party to his nephew's treason. When Gardiner accused Cranmer of heresy, Henry sternly rebuked him and ordered him to go and beg the archbishop's pardon. Later that year Henry went to war with France, staying in that country for six months. He took Gardiner and Norfolk with him and left Catherine as regent. With their enemies out of the way and the queen in charge, heaven appeared to be smiling upon the Reformers.

The following year, 1545, Henry returned and Gardiner made another attempt to overthrow Cranmer. Gardiner and members of the Privy Council accused him of having 'infected the whole realm with his unsavoury doctrines till three parts of England were become abominable heretics' and asked that Cranmer be sent to the Tower. The story is well depicted by Shakespeare in his *Henry VIII*. The king saw Cranmer and gave him his own ring as the warrant to appeal to him. When the Privy Council refused to listen to Cranmer after they had accused him, he presented the ring. The councillors recognized their defeat and surrendered the matter into the king's hands. Henry sharply rebuked them all and declared that he thought that he had men of wisdom in his Council, instead of which they had shown themselves to be fools. Cranmer was his most faithful subject and the primate of all England, while they had treated him as if he were a peasant.

Henry's health deteriorated as 1546 began and he suffered severe leg pains. His temper grew worse and it broke with fresh severity on the most zealous Reformers. Dr Crome, an old friend of Latimer, was brought before the Council for a sermon in which he had attacked the doctrine of purgatory. Crome, powerful in logic, was, like Bilney, weak in other ways and he recanted. The Council then looked for those who had supported Crome and the chief man they wanted was Latimer. Whether the milder regime with the queen as regent had induced him to return to London in 1544 we cannot say, but he was definitely there in the spring of 1546.

Latimer was arrested and on 13 May was brought before the Privy Council where he was accused by Tunstall and Gardiner. Despite his age, Latimer's wits were as sharp as ever and his shrewd answers to their questions left them 'as wise as we were before'. They were unable to get him to confess anything treasonable or heretical and it would appear that he was brought before Henry. As he proved to be immovable, Latimer was sent to the Tower where he remained until Henry's death.

* * * * * *

When Henry was not long for this world, he left a deep

blot on his name by his treatment of a most heroic lady, Anne Askew. She came from a good family but had been driven from home because of her love for the Scriptures, for which her husband hated her. Anne appears to have been a friend of the queen and of other ladies in court who loved the 'new learning'. They met together in the queen's apartment to pray. Also, one of the Reformers often came secretly to expound the Bible.

In March Anne was arrested and Bishop Bonner questioned her on her faith. She was sent to prison but later released. In June, however, the Privy Council summoned her to appear and Gardiner questioned her closely concerning the sacrament, trying to get her to confess that in it there was 'flesh, blood and bone'. For a week she was subjected to a rigorous examination, mostly by the cunning Gardiner. She answered the questions clearly and well but longed to speak with Latimer, now a prisoner in the Tower.

Anne was tried again at the Guildhall and defended herself well, giving scriptural answers. 'That which you call your God, it is a piece of bread,' she said, 'and for more proof thereof let it but lie in the box three months and it will be mouldy. . . .' Anne was condemned to be burnt but they hoped to implicate others by getting her to confess. As she refused, she was taken to the Tower and tortured on the rack, Wriothesley, the Lord Chancellor, himself using this abominable instrument on her. Apart from its barbarity, this was illegal and, while Henry made no effort to save Anne, he was angry that she had been tortured.

The rack dislocated Anne's bones and she was unable to walk, so she was carried to the stake. A pardon was offered to her if she would recant but she answered bravely, 'I came not hither to deny my Lord and Master,' after which she died courageously in the kindled flames. As Bishop Ryle says, 'The Romish doctrine of the *real presence* strikes at the very root of the gospel, and is the very citadel and keep of popery.'[2] Any who attack it are in grave danger when Rome

2. J. C. Ryle, *Five English Reformers*, p.30.

is in power.

Elated by his success with Anne Askew, Gardiner decided to shoot for bigger game. Who better than the queen? If she fell the Reformation might well fall with her. As we have seen, Catherine had been holding private conferences in her chambers where her ladies-in-waiting gathered to listen to the exposition of Scripture by one of her chaplains. Henry had always ignored these meetings, although it was clear that Catherine was an evangelical Christian like Anne Askew. When she saw that Henry did not interfere, Catherine became bolder, since her one desire was to make the truth known to her husband.

Gardiner and his friends approached the king and insinuated that Catherine used her freedom to read and write heretical works. They had to be cautious as Henry's temper was becoming even more unpredictable. At first they failed and were about to give up when they found an unexpected ally. The ulcer on Henry's leg burst causing him acute pain. He became gloomy, passionate and burst into fits of rage. Since Catherine could see that he was rapidly approaching his end, she became even more concerned to try and bring him to put his trust in Christ. She spoke one evening in the presence of Gardiner and Wriothesley, and offended Henry. He was angry at 'women becoming such clerks' and that he, the 'defender of the faith', should be 'taught by his wife in his old age'.

Gardiner seized his opportunity, determined to get rid of Catherine. Henry had rid himself of four queens, why not persuade him to dispose of a fifth? Catherine's life hung by a thread but she was warned of her danger when one of her ladies brought to her a bill of indictment against her, signed by the king, that had been found in the palace grounds. Catherine fainted and nearly died of shock. The king's physician was sent for, who confirmed that the king had indeed signed this paper. He advised her to submit humbly to the king and so obtain his pardon. By careful flattery and diplomacy, Catherine succeeded in making her peace with Henry and when, the next day, Wriothesley appeared, the king called him 'beast, fool, arrant knave'. The plot recoiled on the heads of the conspirators. Gardiner was removed from the Privy Council and from the list of the king's executors, and forbidden ever to appear before Henry again.

The Duke of Norfolk, the other great enemy of the Reformers, was extremely jealous of Jane Seymour's relatives, whom Henry had raised to the peerage. Hearing of a plot hatched against them by Norfolk, Henry put him and his son, the Earl of Surrey, in the Tower. The king feared anything that might threaten his young son and they were charged with trying 'to get the lord prince into their hands after his [Henry's] death'. Surrey was tried and executed on 21 January 1547 but because Norfolk, as a duke, had to be tried by Parliament by a bill of attainder, there was delay. This saved his life.

Henry was rapidly approaching his end but until a few hours before his death no one had the courage to tell him. At last Sir Anthony Denny took courage and told him that, humanly speaking, there was no hope, and advised him to prepare for death. Henry confessed various sins — it is said that he even referred to his sin against Anne Boleyn. Denny suggested that some clergyman should be sent for. 'If I see anyone, it must be Archbishop Cranmer,' Henry said.

When Cranmer arrived Henry was too far gone to speak, but he stretched out his hand to him. The primate exhorted him to put all his trust in Christ. 'Give me some token with your eyes or hand that you trust in the Lord,' Cranmer said. Henry wrung Cranmer's hand as hard as he could and shortly afterwards breathed his last. He died at 2 a.m. on 28 January 1547 at the age of fifty-six. He had reigned thirty-seven years and nine months.

15. *Roving preacher*

1547 — 1553

'The king is dead, long live the king!' Latimer's heart must have rejoiced when these cries echoed to him in the Tower. Young Edward, the 'boy king', was wholeheartedly in favour of the Reformation. Now that the throne was his the future looked brighter than it had ever done before.

In his will Henry had entrusted the affairs of England to a Privy Council until Edward became of age. He was only in his tenth year when his father died. One member of the Council was the Marquis of Hertford, Edward's uncle, whom the other members of the Council appointed as Protector of the Realm with the title of the Duke of Somerset. A few days later Wriothesley, the brutal chancellor, was deprived of his office and the danger from the Catholics was greatly lessened. While England waited with bated breath to see how the Reformers would proceed, it was to the credit of the Protector and the Council that they sent none of their enemies to the scaffold or the stake.

The dangers to the Reformers were not only from Rome. Some of the more zealous Protestants also wished to act in a violent way. Even before Henry's burial the churchwardens and curates of St Martin's Church, Ironmonger Lane, London, had to be brought before the Council for destroying the images of saints and the crucifix over the rood screen. They had broken the law but received a mitigated sentence, very different from the one which Henry would have given. This showed England the course the Council would take concerning the Reformation. The next month Dr Nicholas Ridley preached before the court on Ash Wednesday and denounced, as Latimer had done, the use of images and holy water.

On Henry's death, a general pardon had been proclaimed

Edward VI. *(Reproduced by courtesy of the National Portrait Gallery.)*

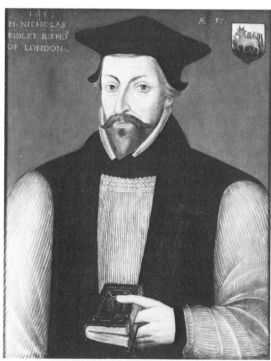

Nicholas Ridley. *(Reproduced by courtesy of the National Portrait Gallery.)*

which released Latimer. Worcester now had another bishop, unworthy of the office that Latimer had once held, but the latter had no desire to be restored to his old see. With declining health, he felt his age. He had proved, too, that his gifts qualified him for the work of a preacher rather than that of a bishop and administrator of ecclesiastical matters. While many wanted him either to resume his old see or else to accept another when it became vacant, he firmly refused. 'He was better fitted for the pulpit than the consistory' says one writer. Latimer did the work of an evangelist and his years of silence had given a depth and maturity to his preaching that made him the greatest preacher of his day, a man who could reach the hearts of all classes of English people.

Wherever Latimer preached, large crowds gathered to listen. His quaint but animated eloquence made a deep impression on the hearts and minds of his hearers. When he was called to preach before the court, a pulpit had to be erected in the king's garden in order to provide enough space for the crowd that thronged to hear him. Later, when he preached in St Margaret's Church, Westminster, the people crushed in and broke the pews.

Latimer was regarded as the apostle of the English Reformation and all recognized that he was not only the ruthless enemy of the superstitions and heresies of Rome, but also a stern preacher against the social vices and sins of his age. As one modern writer says, 'He was the St James of early Protestantism', a man concerned with both sound doctrine and sound living. Faith and works went hand in hand in his thought and preaching. Nor did Latimer flatter the gentry. 'By yeomen's sons the faith of Christ is and hath been maintained chiefly,' he stated bluntly in one sermon. But we must not expect to find much doctrinal teaching in his sermons. He was essentially a practical preacher, hence his popularity. Cranmer and Ridley give us the details of the theological tenets of the English Reformers.

Latimer, together with Taylor, Parker and other gifted preachers, received licences to preach anywhere in England. The Council were cautious with their plans and decided to progress slowly with the work of reform. A Book of Twelve Homilies was compiled, dealing with the use of Scripture, the nature of faith, man's misery by sin, redemption by Christ and other subjects. Some homilies were by Cranmer but it is believed that others were partly or totally the work of Latimer. While this cannot be proved, it is quite in keeping with his gifts. He often stayed with Cranmer at Lambeth and crowds tried to reach him to ask for help on different matters. Latimer was grateful for his faithful Swiss servant, Augustine Bernher, who took much of the burden from his shoulders.

The clergy received orders to preach faithfully to their flocks and encourage them in works of faith, mercy and charity. Pilgrimages, tapers, praying upon beads and other superstitions were to be discouraged. Images were to be taken down and a chapter of the New Testament was to be read publicly every Sunday morning in church and a chapter of the Old Testament in the afternoon. Processions round churches and many other Catholic traditions encouraged by Henry were banned.

In spite of all these steps in the right direction, one great abuse remained — the mass. But the Council already had ideas about reforming this, too. Men like Bonner and Gardiner could not keep silent as they saw the Reformers regaining their lost ground and even preparing to make further advances towards the New Testament position on most basic doctrines. Bonner was brought before the Council and then sent to the Fleet prison. Gardiner refused to obey the orders given regarding the reading of Scripture and also objected to the homilies. He proved stubborn and refused to obey the Council, so was sent to join Bonner in the Fleet.

When Parliament assembled in November 1547 it repealed all the cruel laws of Henry VIII, abolished the Six Articles, and even the old laws against the Lollards. While toleration as we understand it was then unknown, the removal of all the persecuting laws marked real progress. But the greatest step forward was the reformation of the mass. While the majority of the Reformers in England were as yet unprepared to abandon teaching that they had absorbed from childhood, they felt that the ordinary man or woman had as much right to partake of the cup of wine at the Lord's Supper as had the priest. It was accordingly ordered that the ordinance should be administered in 'both kinds', and no person who humbly and devoutly desired it should be denied. Although the teaching concerning the sacrament still differed from that of most Continental Reformers, England had at last fallen into line with Scripture regarding the administering of the Lord's Supper.

One of Latimer's best-known sermons, the 'Sermon of the Plough', gives us an example of his preaching in Edward's reign, as well as showing how his thoughts were moving concerning the Lord's Supper. 'I liken preaching to a ploughman's labour,' Latimer said, preaching at Paul's Cross in January 1548, 'and a prelate to a ploughman. . . a prelate is that man whosoever he be, that hath a flock to be taught of him; whosoever hath any spiritual charge in the faithful congregation, and whosoever he be that hath the cure of souls. And well may the preacher and the ploughman be likened together. . . for as the ploughman first setteth forth his plough, and then tilleth his land, and breaketh it in furrows. . . so the prelate, the preacher, hath many diverse offices to do. He hath first a busy work to bring his parishioners to a right faith, as Paul calleth it, and not a swerving faith; to a faith that embraceth Christ and trusteth to His merits; a lively faith, a justifying faith, a faith that maketh a man righteous, without respect of works. . . .'

Latimer expounded both the work of the preacher, and the response that God expects from those that hear the Word. He pointed out how many prelates in the past had been 'unpreaching prelates, lording loiterers and idle ministers'. Not only those in the past, Latimer said pointedly, but some in England today preferred to lord it over the people rather than preach. 'And now I would ask a strange question: who is the most diligentest bishop and prelate in all England, that passeth all the rest in doing his office? I can tell, for I know him who it is; I know him well. . . . And will ye know who it is? I will tell you: it is the devil. He is the most diligent preacher of all the others: he is never out of his diocese; he is never from his cure; ye shall never find him unoccupied. . . . When the devil is resident and hath his plough going, there away with books, and up with candles; away with Bibles, and up with beads; away with the light of the gospel, and up with the light of candles. . . . There never was such a preacher in England as he is.'

Then Latimer showed how his convictions had changed. 'This is the mark at which the devil shooteth, to evacuate [make of no effect] the cross of Christ, and to mingle [confuse] the institution of the Lord's Supper: and these fifteen hundred years he hath been a doer, only purposing to evacuate Christ's death, and to make it of small efficacy and virtue. For whereas Christ, according as the serpent was lifted up in the wilderness, so would He Himself be exalted, that thereby as many as trusteth in Him should have salvation; but the devil would none of that: they [the Catholics] would have us saved by a daily oblation. . . but Christ is a continual sacrifice in effect, fruit, operation and virtue. . . to them that believe and trust in Him, as He was fifteen hundred years ago when He was crucified. Then let us trust upon His only death and look for none other sacrifice propitiatory. . . . What other oblation have we to make but of obedience, of good living, of good works, and of helping our neighbours? . . . But the devil, by the help of that Italian bishop yonder, his chaplain, hath laboured by all means that he might to frustrate the death of Christ and the merits of His passion.'

Language like this stirred the hearts of most men in Latimer's time and weakened the grip that the old superstitions still had on many people's minds. His enforced silence had purged his mind from much of the old teaching and we see, too, how his opinion on the question of the mass had changed dramatically. He still held to transubstantiation for a few more months, but no longer accepted it as a propitiatory sacrifice. In March 1548 the Council issued an 'Order of the Communion' in *English*. It retained the rites of the mass but promised further reform, and it was the foundation for the communion service as found in the Book of

Common Prayer. Some of the changes may have been suggested by Latimer; without question his preaching moved many of the Council as well as the common people.

Young King Edward loved the Reformation and it was only to be expected that a man whose words moved the crowds should be asked to preach before the king. In 1548 Latimer preached seven sermons in Lent at the Palace of St James, Westminster. A pulpit was set up in the privy-garden and while the garden was crowded with courtiers, the young king listened from a window. As usual Latimer slanted his sermon for his congregation and with an audience of courtiers he dwelt on the vices and sins of the rich.

In one of his sermons Latimer dwelt on his favourite topic — the necessity for preaching. His emphasis on this was unique among English Reformers but it elevated Latimer to a place above his fellow Reformers. They had seen the life-giving power of Scripture but failed to take it to its logical conclusion: 'Faith comes from what is heard, and what is heard comes by the preaching of Christ.' The place that baptism occupied in the church still confused the other Reformers and many ascribed to it the same regenerating power that Rome does. But this was not the case with Latimer: ' "By the Word of the living God", by the Word of God preached and opened — thus cometh our new birth.'[1]

In 1548 Latimer had preached on 'Restitution', an unsavoury subject with courtiers who, for the most part, all had their hands stained with ill-gotten goods. When he preached in 1550 he told them that, 'One good man took remorse of conscience, and acknowledged himself to me that he had deceived the king; and willing he was to make restitution: and so the first Lent came to my hands twenty pounds to be restored to the king's use. . . . Well, the next Lent came three hundred and twenty pounds more; . . . this Lent came one hundred and four score pounds ten shillings, which I have paid and delivered this day to the king's Council.'

The 'good man' referred to was John Bradford and during

1. *Latimer's Sermons*, Parker Society edition, p. 203.

the French wars he had been involved in business whereby the king had been defrauded. Bradford heard Latimer preach and was so conscience-stricken that on Latimer's advice he wrote to the person concerned and warned him that restitution must be made or else he would write to Somerset. Latimer acted as go-between and paid the conscience money to the Council. Latimer also saw Bradford's talent and ability as a Christian minister. On his advice Bradford went to Cambridge to prepare for the ministry. He later received an appointment as one of the six royal chaplains with a roving commission to preach the doctrines of the Reformation. The effect of Latimer's sermon on Bradford is sufficient to demonstrate that he preached with both eloquence and power from above.

Cranmer had the pious hope that he might be able, with the help of the great Continental Reformers, to set up a truly Reformed Christian church which would be firmly evangelical and based only on Scripture, and would include all the Reformed churches in Europe. Partly because of this idea and partly because the students of England needed better teachers, many of the best Reformed Continental divines received invitations to England. Melancthon was unable to come but Bucer, Peter Martyr, Paul Fagius and John a Lasco came with others and Lambeth Palace became the centre where they met.

Through the influence of the Continental Reformers more reforms were undertaken. Latimer must have been overjoyed at fellowship with Christians from other lands, but the greatest result that it produced was the abandonment by Cranmer and Latimer of their belief in transubstantiation, probably in September 1548. In a letter to Bullinger dated 28 September 1548, Traheron stated, 'Latimer has come over to our opinion respecting the true doctrine of the eucharist, together with the Archbishop of Canterbury. . . who heretofore seemed Lutherans.'[2] At the end of the year many prelates and divines met at Windsor to revise the service books and

2. *Zurich Letters*, p. 322.

prepare a Book of Common Prayer in English. This, of course, had to be passed by both the House of Commons and the House of Lords. The subject of the Lord's Supper took much time and long debates ensued. Bonner and Tunstall were the leaders of the Catholic viewpoint (Gardiner was still in prison) and opposed it vehemently. After two months the Prayer Book received the royal sanction and became law in the spring of 1549. Parliament also repealed the laws enforcing the celibacy of the clergy. The Catholic clergy strongly opposed this also.

In January 1549 Somerset received a request from the Commons which asked him to restore Latimer to his old see of Worcester. But Latimer refused this as he was convinced that his work was to be 'the king's preacher'. He preached at least twice on Sundays and studied diligently. He rose early, at 2 a.m., summer and winter for prayer and study. Latimer knew well that much needed to be done in England as reform was only partial. He said when preaching before Edward, 'We have the ministration of His Word; we are yet well: but the house is not clean swept yet.'

These were timely words of Latimer's since, apart from dangers from the Catholics, the Reformers faced new threats, now that they were succeeding in some measure. Many nominal Christians paid mere lip service to the teachings of the preachers and of Scripture, and their lives were an outrage to the doctrines they professed to follow. They considered an orthodox creed a substitute for a holy life. With a young king, there were many nobles and gentry who assented to the popular creed in order to gain his favour. Latimer was as merciless in his preaching against such people as he was against hardened Catholics.

The old sin of simony (selling spiritual offices for money), which had been practised by Rome for centuries, again became common. It reached such proportions that many benefices were sold to laymen, and the churches, uncared for by any minister, soon had dust-covered pulpits. Finally a bill was introduced in 1553 which stated that no one should hold ecclesiastical office unless he was at least a deacon, but the

Commons had sunk so low that it threw out the bill. With these facts before us we begin to appreciate the enormous task that faced Latimer and the other Reformers.

The immoral living of many people of all levels of society was not the only problem that the Reformers had to face. When toleration comes in any degree it inevitably brings with it heresies from those who pride themselves on their 'private interpretation' of Scripture. In April 1549 one Joan Bocher, or Joan of Kent, appeared before a commission comprised of Cranmer, Ridley, Latimer and twenty others. This woman, confused by Anabaptist speculations, denied the true Incarnation of Christ. Cranmer and the others reasoned with her but she remained obstinate and even taunted them on their ignorance of Scripture. For a sixteenth-century woman, Joan was quick with her replies: 'It was not long ago,' she said, 'since you burned Anne Askew for a piece of bread,' (none of her judges had been involved in Anne's trial) 'and yet came yourselves soon after to believe and profess the same doctrine for which you burned her. And now, forsooth, you will needs burn me for a piece of flesh [our Lord's body], and in the end you will come to believe this also, when you have read the Scriptures and understand them.'

Joan was excommunicated but remained immovable. She was condemned and placed in prison. It was hoped that calm reflection might change her mind but nothing could move her and on 2 May 1550 she died at the stake. Her death has left a black mark on the Reformers and shows that toleration, as we understand it, was then unknown. England had just emerged from medieval darkness and, while this does not excuse their action, it does help to explain it.

The reforms were not all welcomed. The first Book of Common Prayer was initially used on Whit Sunday, 9 June 1549. Some of the people in Devon rose in revolt and insisted that they did not want a new service or the Bible and demanded the restoration of the old Latin service and the Six Articles. Trouble also arose in Wiltshire, Sussex, Hampshire and Yorkshire. But much of the disturbance in these other counties was basically connected with injustices from the nobles as they had enclosed land that had always been common property.

In the autumn of 1549 Somerset, the Protector, fell. He was charged with treason and sent to the Tower. He had always been a zealous Reformer; now it was hoped by the Roman party that the Duke of Northumberland, a secret Catholic, would succeed him and restore the old Latin service and ceremonies. Their hopes were not realized. Northumberland willingly sacrificed his creed to gain the place offered to him and became the new Protector. He remained a Catholic at heart but threw in his lot with the Reformers and deceived most of them, who believed him to be an ardent Reformer.

The Parliament that sat from November 1549 to January 1550 carried out more reforms. All images, apart from those on tombs, were to be broken and defaced to prevent people from using them for superstitious purposes. The authorities demanded that all the old service books, missals and ordinals should be handed over to be destroyed or defaced so that they might never be used again. It is worth noting that most bishops opposed these reforms and when the Reformed Ordinal was passed, which included the service for the ordination of priests and deacons and removed most of the Romish ceremonies, only six bishops voted for it. The votes of the temporal peers carried it through the House of Lords. The majority of bishops remained Roman Catholic at heart.

Early in 1550 Latimer became seriously ill and it was feared that he would die. For a time his life hung in the balance, but he recovered and took up his duties as court preacher in Lent. He appears to have preached only one day, morning and afternoon, on Monday, 10 March. Possibly his health prevented more than this. He seemed to realize that his days were numbered and preached zealously on the immorality and bribery of his day. All evil appeared to him to be summed up in one phrase, 'the love of money', and he preached strongly and solemnly against covetousness to both king and court.

John Hooper, who had returned from Zurich, also preached before Edward in Lent, and was offered the see of

Gloucester. Hooper refused as he objected to the Oath of Supremacy to the king and he condemned the episcopal clothes and ceremonies used in consecration which he declared to be 'popish'. Hooper's time in Switzerland had shown him how much the English church still needed reform, but it is to his discredit that he spoke harshly of the reforming bishops in England. He had enjoyed greater privileges than they as he learnt from the Continental Reformers and he should have made allowance for the slower growth of his English associates. When the king struck out the offending oath and promised to get rid of the displeasing vestments, Hooper then agreed to accept the bishopric, but others had been angered by his unbending attitude. Parliament had only recently authorized the form of ordination and Ridley, now Bishop of London, took an equally firm stand, insisting that the law must be obeyed without any alterations.

Angry confrontations followed, to the grief of all Reformers. Peter Martyr and Bucer both censured Hooper but he refused to yield. Despite the fact that the Council confined him to his house and forbad him to preach, he published a *Confession and Protestation* repeating all the statements that had caused the quarrel. The Council then sent him to the Fleet prison. In March 1551 he submitted and was consecrated as bishop with all the ceremonies to which he had objected. This left much bitterness in the church and it might have been better if Hooper, like John Knox, had declined an office about which he had scruples of conscience.

There are two ways of looking at this. One is that since Hooper had such firm and clear views on vestments and oaths and, rightly, believed in bringing everything to the 'touchstone of Scripture', he should not have accepted the bishopric but should have gracefully 'agreed to disagree' with the other Reformers and remained a preacher like Latimer. Alternatively, one could say that he ought to have recognized that his colleagues were less clear and mature in their thinking on the unbiblical vestments and oaths and accordingly given them more time to mature and see the biblical teaching that he stood for. We saw earlier that the Continental

Reformers did this concerning the mass.

Hooper was, in fact, ahead of his time. He was a fore-runner of the Puritans who pressed hard to have these un-biblical practices removed from the Church of England. But England was making slower progress in its Reformation, especially when under Henry's restraining hand, than Germany or Switzerland and Hooper had not allowed for this. We need to remember, too, that in Zurich, where Hooper stayed for part of his exile, the Reformation had finally been decided by the sword. It had not been peaceable but it had been rapid. He may have hoped for faster reform by his action, but this was not to be. While, doctrinally, Hooper was right, he showed a harsh spirit and there is a parallel between Paul in his earlier days when he quarrelled with Barnabas over Mark's behaviour, and Hooper's action. Paul was un-doubtedly right, but he took too harsh a view of the younger and (possibly) weaker Mark. But years later, in his imprison-ment, Paul admitted that Mark was 'very useful to him'. It is pleasant to record that Ridley later acknowledged that Hooper was right and he had been wrong.

Although Latimer played no part in this dispute, it greatly grieved him. It may, too, have contributed towards his fore-bodings that, for a time at least, the Reformation would be overthrown in England and its leaders would perish. He referred to this several times in one sermon. The dispute caused a deep-rooted prejudice to spread among many English people — prejudice against foreign ideas that Hooper had tried to introduce from Switzerland. Many failed to understand what the quarrel was about but from that time they had less confidence in the Reformers. This was largely the result of Hooper's more advanced views.

1552 saw the ratification by Parliament of the second Book of Common Prayer, cleared of most features which offended the Continental Reformers, and the preparation of a series of doctrinal articles for the Church of England. Cranmer drew up forty-two articles after consultation with Ridley and possibly Latimer. They were submitted to the six royal chaplains for revision and in 1553 received the king's approval.

Latimer was no longer the court preacher. Apart from his failing health, it is doubtful if the Council wanted a man who boldly censured their actions. The new Protector disliked him since he was shrewd enough to see through his plans. Latimer and Cranmer both ceased to enjoy their previous esteem. Younger clergy, zealous for the truth, became the leaders and preachers. They were men of great energy, honest and learned, but young and impetuous, unequipped and unqualified to direct the nation in a difficult time. While they preached against Rome many English people were becoming alienated from the Reformation. Clouds were gathering over the country.

From early 1551 Latimer ceased to be the 'king's preacher' and could be said to have retired to the country. His tongue was never idle; he preached wherever he found opportunity except in London. His eloquence appears to have matured with age and what the capital lost the country gained. Many humble folk benefited from the fact that Latimer had fallen from favour with the Protector. Augustine Bernher, his servant, went everywhere with him. He recorded many of Latimer's sermons and had them printed in Elizabeth's reign. As with our Lord, it could be said of Latimer that 'the common people heard him gladly'. As a yeoman's son, Latimer could reach the hearts of peasants.

He also continued to enjoy hospitality from rich friends. Latimer stayed many times with the Dowager Duchess of Suffolk, a zealous supporter of the Reformers, and preached to the servants in her castle at Grimsthorpe, Lincolnshire. He may even have visited Leicestershire and his old friends, since the road from Grimsthorpe to Baxterley passed through that county. We have no evidence of this but it is known that he preached in Lincolnshire, Leicestershire and Warwickshire until Edward's death.

Edward had never been strong. Early in 1552 he had measles and smallpox which greatly weakened him. In 1553 it soon became clear to all that he was dying of consumption. He had always been a sickly youth and now the future of

Protestantism in England appeared to hang on his life. Henry had laid down in his will that Edward was to succeed him and, if he died without children, Mary was to succeed Edward. Mary still remained a fanatical Catholic who had refused to adopt the changes in religion ordered by Parliament. In consequence she was odious to most English Reformers.

The sick young king was grieved at the idea of the Reformation being reversed at his death. When Northumberland presented him with a document leaving the crown to Lady Jane Grey, the eldest granddaughter of the Duke of Suffolk and Mary Tudor, the youngest sister of Henry VIII, Edward willingly signed. This was illegal but Edward was eager to do anything to keep Mary from the throne. Northumberland then hurriedly married his own son, Guildford Dudley, to Lady Jane. Edward, 'God's imp' as he was called, died at Greenwich on 6 July 1553, asking God in his last words to 'defend the nation from papistry' and beseeching Him to 'maintain His true religion'. Edward was not yet sixteen.

At Paul's Cross Bishop Ridley assured the crowds that Lady Jane must be accepted as their lawful queen.

16. 'Such a candle'

'Master Latimer, I bring you an important message. It is from the Lord Chancellor. You are to appear before him immediately.'

Latimer turned slowly. So it had arrived at last. Ever since he learned that Mary had been proclaimed queen in London on 19 July 1553 and the ill-fated Lady Jane Grey, her husband and Northumberland had been confined in the Tower, he had expected such a summons. Gardiner, released from the Tower, was now Lord Chancellor and the whole pattern of power in England had been reversed. Many Englishmen had fled in disguise to Germany or Switzerland and the Continental Protestants had been ordered out of the country.

Latimer was preaching in Warwickshire at the time of Mary's accession and had been warned of the approach of the messenger. Had he so wished, he had ample time to escape. While he was not a man to court martyrdom, he realized that the time had come when a faithful preacher might justifiably expose himself to the risk of death. He had not broken the law or taken any part in the support of Lady Jane Grey, but he enjoyed too great a reputation among the common people to be left undisturbed.

To the amazement of the messenger, Latimer immediately prepared to go to London. 'My friend,' he said, 'you be a welcome messenger to me. And be it known unto you, and to all the world, that I go as willingly to London at this present, being called by my prince to render a reckoning of my doctrine, as ever I was at any place in the world. I doubt not but that God, as He hath made me worthy to preach His Word before two excellent princes, so will He able me to witness the same unto the third, either to her comfort, or discomfort eternally.'[1]

Latimer's servant, Augustine Bernher, who recorded this statement, thought the fact that the messenger then returned to London leaving Latimer to follow, meant that the Council were giving him a chance to escape if he so wished. But Latimer remembered the courage shown by Bilney and Bainham when faced with death. He had weakened once, but he would not do so again. On the way to the Council he passed Smithfield, the customary place for burning heretics. 'Smithfield has long groaned for me,' Latimer remarked.

He was brought before the Privy Council on 13 September 1553 and for 'his seditious demeanour was committed to the Tower, there to remain a close prisoner, having attending upon him one Austy, his servant,' as the Privy Council book records. Latimer had not committed any act of sedition but the word 'seditious' would appear to refer to his personal bearing when he stood before the Council. 'Diotrophes [Gardiner] now of late did ever harp upon unity, unity. "Yea sir," quoth I, "but in verity not in popery. Better is diversity, than a unity in popery." I had nothing again but scornful taunts with commandment to the Tower.'[2]

Latimer was confined with Cranmer and Ridley but in a separate cell. These three men who had done so much to spread the light of the gospel throughout England were left in the Tower and virtually ignored until the following spring. Latimer spent much of his time in prayer and in reading the New Testament. He remained calm and self-possessed and still showed that sense of humour that had marked his preaching. He had made up his mind and his duty to his Lord and the faith that he maintained was clear. He trusted that God would supply the grace and courage to face whatever lay ahead.

As winter set in Latimer and his companions were nearly frozen, but he was not one to take such things lying down.

1. Bernher, *Introduction to Sermons on the Lord's Prayer*.

2. Conference between Ridley and Latimer in Prison. Foxe, *Acts and Monuments*, vol. vii, p. 411.

'Master lieutenant,' he said to the Lord Lieutenant of the Tower, 'you look, I think, that I should burn; but except you let me have some fire, I am like to deceive your expectation, for I am like here to starve for cold.' After this they received better treatment and Bernher brought Latimer news and letters from Ridley and Cranmer. He learnt that in October England had been restored to the same state as it was at Henry's death. Catherine's divorce and all the religious changes made by Edward had been repealed by Parliament. Had all their work been wasted?

The prisoners wisely spent their time in preparing to defend their faith when brought for trial and many letters passed between Latimer, Ridley and Cranmer via their servants. The main doctrine on which they expected to be questioned was what they believed about the mass. As Bishop Ryle says, 'The Romish doctrine of the *real presence* strikes at the very root of the gospel.' 'If they did not believe and admit it, they were burned.'

Mary saw to it that no man went unpunished who had declared her mother's marriage null and void and her illegitimate. Cranmer had led the court which settled this question and Latimer and Ridley had upheld his decision. But neither would Rome let any man go free if he denied the 'sacrifice of the mass'; it was and is the centre of her worship. The queen was convinced that treason and heresy were inseparable but prudence restrained her from violence against Latimer and his associates. She desperately wanted a husband and, from the list of possible bridegrooms, she selected Philip II of Spain. Gardiner, her chancellor, although capable of any cruelty, was too wise to be systematically cruel if it were imprudent. He could see that to bring England back to its state at Henry's death was one thing, but to press on and restore the Roman faith overnight was another. While his counsel prevailed, Mary waited.

But an exile long out of touch with England volunteered to return home and restore the country to a truly Catholic state. The pope created Reginald Pole a cardinal and commissioned him to bring England back to the Holy See. When Pole

joined Mary a drastic purge would take place. The man who
had been commissioned by the pope to open the Council of
Trent and launch the Counter-Reformation would take ruthless steps. But others moved more quickly than Pole. Charles
V, Philip's father, took no chances lest Pole should frustrate
the marriage and put every obstacle in the cardinal's way to
ensure that he did not reach England until Philip and Mary
were married. This took place at Winchester on 6 March
1554. Cardinal Pole eventually reached England in the late
autumn of that year.

In January 1554 Sir Thomas Wyatt rose in revolt with the
men of Kent, crossed the river at Kingston-upon-Thames and
advanced on London. Fighting broke out at Charing Cross
and arrows rattled into the courtyard of Whitehall. While this
was a political revolt led by disaffected gentry, it meant that
if Wyatt succeeded, Latimer would be freed. But very soon
Latimer learned from Bernher that Wyatt had been trapped
at Temple Bar and was imprisoned. Suddenly the Tower became crowded with prisoners.

One advantage came from this. Latimer, Cranmer and
Ridley were herded into one cell, together with Bradford,
Latimer's youngest convert. This gave them the opportunity
of fellowship. They read the Bible together and discussed important doctrinal questions. They read and re-read the teachings of Christ and the apostles on the Lord's Supper as they
knew this would be the key question at their trial. John
Bradford was tough-minded and his presence boosted the
morale of the other prisoners, especially Latimer who had a
harsh jailor. The prisoners learned that Lady Jane Grey had
been executed and that Mary had imprisoned her half-sister
Elizabeth in the Tower, and that the Spaniards were
clamouring for her execution, too.

For two months Latimer, Cranmer, Ridley and Bradford
enjoyed their fellowship and then news arrived that all,
except Bradford, must go to Oxford for trial. Preparations
were made at Oxford for a public disputation. Cranmer,
Ridley and Latimer would be faced by the theological glad-
iators of the two universities, who hoped to discredit them

openly to the shame and disgrace of all Protestants. Heresy
was the charge now levied against them. As one writer says,
this was done 'so that it might appear that she [Mary] did
not act out of revenge'.

The prisoners arrived at Oxford at the end of March and
were locked in the town jail, the Bocardo. They had been
allowed to take with them such books as they could carry.
On Friday, 13 April, the commissioners appointed by Oxford
and Cambridge met, under the leadership of Dr Weston, and
the next day the trial began at St Mary's Church. Gardiner
had drawn up three articles to which each prisoner was to
subscribe. Needless to say, they all dealt with the mass. The
first stated that the true and natural body of Christ was really
present in the sacrament after the words of consecration; the
second that at that point there was no other substance in
the elements, and the third that the mass was a propitiatory
sacrifice for the sins of the living and the dead. The doctrine
of the mass was the acid test of orthodoxy as it still is in the
Roman Catholic Church today. If the prisoners denied this
they were heretics; if they confessed it, Rome had won a
victory.

They were brought in separately, first Cranmer, then
Ridley and finally Latimer. They all denied the articles drawn
up by Gardiner and were told to prepare to submit their
opinions in writing the next week. Cranmer was to appear on
Monday, Ridley on Tuesday, and Latimer on Wednesday.
Cranmer did not succeed very well in his debate, Ridley
proved a tougher antagonist than Cranmer, but, on the
Wednesday, Latimer was in a very weak state and read a
profession of faith. When challenged by his accusers he
claimed that transubstantiation was a historical invention.
Altogether Latimer gave no satisfaction to his accusers and
his stubbornness irritated them. After the prisoners had been
brought before the court, they were kept apart. Cranmer was
sent to the Bocardo, Ridley to an alderman's house, and
Latimer to the bailiff's. From now on no further opportunity
would be given to them to help one another.

On Friday, 20 April they were given a final chance to
submit and, after their refusal, were declared heretics and

excommunicated. On hearing the sentence, Latimer said, 'I thank God most heartily that He hath prolonged my life to this end, that I may in this case glorify God by that kind of death.' The prolocutor replied, 'If *you* go to heaven in this faith, then *I* will never come hither, as I am thus persuaded.' The Reformers returned to their respective prisons and all three expected a speedy death at the stake, instead of which they remained in jail for a further sixteen months before they were again sent for.

During this time great changes had taken place. Pole had reached England and the papal authority had been restored. Mary longed desperately for a child but she remained barren. She was convinced that her failure to conceive was due to God's judgement; He was punishing England for its heresies and so the fires of Smithfield began. While she lived the faggots never ceased to blaze and altogether two hundred and eighty-five people perished for their faith.

Latimer remained a pillar of strength to the other two. Through Bernher, he encouraged Ridley and Cranmer in their prisons. Ridley wrote prolifically but Latimer spent his time in prayer and reading his Bible, which became increasingly precious to him. His most earnest prayer was for the restoration of the gospel in England once again. Bernher records that he often heard Latimer repeat these words 'once again', 'once again'.

In September 1555 a new body of commissioners, led by Brooks, Bishop of Gloucester, met at Oxford. The prisoners were again examined separately, Latimer last of all. His age and poor state of health gave him a slight advantage and he was allowed to sit to answer the charges and, fortunately, the proceedings were short. Latimer remained firm. The charges were virtually unchanged. Did he believe that the bread became the real body of Christ and was it a real sacrifice when the priest spoke the words of consecration? Latimer refused to yield and when he asked permission to speak the judge refused, mainly because Ridley had been given permission and had achieved a measure of success, making his prosecutor look foolish. Fearing a repetition of that scene the judges told Latimer that he was a

condemned heretic and it was unlawful for them to listen to
him. One of them said, 'Your stubbornness. . .will do you no
good when a faggot is in your beard.' That 'faggot' soon
came.

Latimer and Ridley were degraded from their offices as
priests and, on 16 October 1555, were brought to the 'town
ditch' on the north side of Oxford, close to Balliol College.
On the way they had to pass the Bocardo where Cranmer was
imprisoned. He was brought out to see them pass but forbidden to speak to them. Ridley came first, well-dressed and
dignified, and Latimer followed in threadbare garments,
joking a little about his slow progress.

The vice-chancellor, the mayor and many dignitaries of the
city and university were present. There was also an adequate
guard. The authorities dared not take any chances as Latimer
and Ridley had gained many sympathizers during their imprisonment and a large crowd had gathered to witness the
execution.

The two friends greeted each other with joy. They had not
met face to face since their time in the Bocardo. Latimer and
Ridley prayed together and talked quietly until it was time
for the regulation sermon, preached to all heretics. This was
preached by Richard Smith, who had professed to be a
Protestant during Edward's reign but had become a turncoat.
Smith told them that they were committing suicide because
they refused to recant and accept the queen's pardon. He exhorted them to return to the unity of the Roman church.

Latimer and Ridley begged Lord Williams, who presided at
the burning, for permission to reply to Smith but he refused.
They accepted his decision and stood firm. If they wavered
or faltered in their courage the cause of the Reformation in
England could become desperate. Might not people doubt the
very gospel that they had preached? They knew that their
salvation was through faith alone and did not depend on
belonging to the church of Rome. The salvation of countless
men and women might depend on the way in which they
faced death, so they quietly prepared for the fire. As
Spurgeon has written, 'Is not patient silence the best reply to

The burning of Latimer and Ridley, from Foxe's *Acts and Monuments*. (*Reproduced by courtesy of the Bodleian Library.*)

a gainsaying world? Calm endurance answers some questions
infinitely more conclusively than the loftiest eloquence. The
best apologists for Christianity in the early days were its
martyrs. The anvil breaks a host of hammers by quietly
bearing their blows.'

Ridley distributed his garments and also some mementos
among his weeping friends and relatives. Latimer just allowed
himself to be undressed, 'and, being stripped into his shroud,
he seemed as comely a person to them that were present, as
one should likely see. . . '. Many men who stood there wept.
The smith fastened the two Reformers to the stake with a
chain and the faggots were piled around them. George
Shipside, Ridley's brother-in-law, brought a bag of gun-
powder for each of them which he hoped would shorten their
sufferings. 'Then they brought a faggot kindled with fire, and
laid it down at Ridley's feet, to whom Latimer then spoke in
this manner: *"Be of good comfort, Master Ridley, and play
the man. We shall this day light such a candle, by God's
grace, in England, as I trust shall never be put out."'* [3]

The flames leapt up around them and Latimer cried,
'Father of heaven, receive my soul!' He died swiftly,
probably from suffocation, but Ridley suffered agonies from
a slow fire. The dreadful spectacle filled the onlookers with
horror. The crowd wept and lamented and at least one
Catholic was converted outright by the terrible sight.

'Precious in the sight of the Lord is the death of His saints.'

---

3. Foxe, *Acts and Monuments*, vol vii, p.550.

Select bibliography

Trevelyan, G. M., *History of England*, Longmans, Green, 1926.

Trevelyan, G. M., *England in the Age of Wycliffe*, Longmans, Green, 1899.

Trevelyan, G. M., *English Social History*, Longmans, Green, 1942.

Bindoff, S. T., *Tudor England*, Pelican, 1950.

Fraser, Antonia, (ed.), *The Lives of Kings and Queens of England*, Weidenfeld & Nicolson, 1975.

Atkinson, James, *The Great Light*, Paternoster Press, 1968.

Lindsay, T. M., *History of the Reformation*, (2 vols), T. & T. Clark, 1906 and 1907.

D'Aubigné, J. H. Merle, *History of the Reformation*, Religious Tract Society, 1846.

D'Aubigné, J. H. Merle, *The Reformation in England*, Banner of Truth Trust, 1962 and 1963.

Loane, M. L., *Pioneers of the Reformation in England*, Church Book Room Press, 1964.

Edwards, B. H., *God's Outlaw*, Evangelical Press, 1976.

Darby, H. S., *Hugh Latimer*, Epworth Press, 1953.

Demaus, Robert, *Hugh Latimer*, Religious Tract Society, 1869.

Select Sermons and Letters of Hugh Latimer, Religious Tract Society, 1830.

Loades, D.M., *The Oxford Martyrs*, B. T. Batsford, 1970.

Foxe, John, *Acts and Monuments of the Christian Church*, R. B. Seeley & W. Burnside, 1838.

Ryle, J. C., *Five English Reformers*, Banner of Truth Trust, 1960.

Poole-Connor, E. J., *Evangelicalism in England*, H. E. Walter, 1966.

Boettner, Loraine, *Roman Catholicism*, Presbyterian and
    Reformed Publishing Co., 1962.
Bettenson, H., (ed.), *Documents of the Christian Church*,
    Oxford University Press, 1943.
Underwood, A. C., *A History of the English Baptists*, Carey
    Kingsgate Press Ltd, 1947.

General index